Copyright

The Good Energy Cookbook: Boost Your Energy Level with Every Bite.

All rights reserved.

No part of this book may be reproduced, distributed, or transmitted in any form or by any means, including photocopying, recording, or other electronic or mechanical methods, without the prior written permission of the publisher, except in the case of brief quotations embodied in critical reviews and certain other non-commercial uses permitted by copyright law.

The content, recipes, and images in The Good Energy Cookbook are the intellectual property of the author and are protected by copyright and other applicable intellectual property laws. Unauthorized use, reproduction, or distribution of any part of this book, in any format, is strictly prohibited and may result in legal action being taken.

This book is provided "as is," without warranty of any kind, express or implied, including but not limited to the warranties of merchantability, fitness for a particular purpose, or non-infringement. The author and publisher disclaim any and all liability for damages of any kind arising from the use of this book, including but not limited to indirect, incidental, or consequential damages.

Disclaimer

The information and recipes provided in The Good Energy Cookbook are intended solely for informational and inspirational purposes. The content in this book is not a substitute for professional medical advice, diagnosis, or treatment, and should not be considered as such. While the recipes and dietary recommendations are crafted to support a healthy lifestyle, they are not tailored to meet specific medical needs or dietary requirements of any individual.

We strongly encourage you to consult with a healthcare professional, registered dietitian, or nutritionist before making any significant changes to your diet, especially if you have existing health conditions, dietary restrictions, or are on medication. Every person's nutritional needs and health situations are unique, and it is crucial to seek personalized guidance from a qualified professional to ensure that any dietary adjustments align with your health goals and medical history.

Please be aware that certain ingredients used in the recipes, such as nuts, dairy, gluten, or spices, may cause allergies or intolerances in some individuals. Always check the ingredients and nutritional content of the recipes, and adjust or omit them as needed to suit your personal dietary needs and preferences. If you experience any adverse reactions, discontinue the use of that recipe and seek medical attention immediately.

The author, publisher, and any contributors of The Good Energy Cookbook are not responsible or liable for any health-related issues or complications that may arise from the use of the recipes or recommendations in this book. All users of this book assume full responsibility for their dietary and lifestyle choices. Additionally, the information contained in this book may not be complete, accurate, or up-to-date in light of new research and developments in nutrition and health. As such, we advise you to keep informed and consult reliable sources for the latest guidance.

By using The Good Energy Cookbook, you acknowledge and agree that you are doing so at your own risk. The author and publisher disclaim all liability for any potential damage, loss, or injury resulting directly or indirectly from the use or misuse of the content and recipes provided in this book. Always prioritize your health and well-being by seeking professional advice when necessary.

Table of Contents

INTRODUCTION 7

    The Power of Metabolism: Fueling Limitless Health 7

    How Food Affects Energy and Well-Being 8

    The Science of Good Energy: Metabolism Explained 9

    What You'll Find in This Cookbook 10

CHAPTER 1: UNDERSTANDING METABOLISM 11

    What Is Metabolism? 12

    Metabolic Types: How Your Body Processes Energy 13

    Common Myths About Metabolism 13

    Role of Hormones In Metabolism 15

CHAPTER 2: SUPERFOODS FOR METABOLISM 19

    What Are Superfoods? And Why Do They Matter For Metabolism? 19

    Top Superfoods For Metabolism 20

    Incorporating Superfoods in Daily Life 21

CHAPTER 3: LOWERING LDL CHOLESTEROL 23

    Understanding LDL Cholesterol & Its Impact On Health 23

    Foods & Nutrients That Lower LDL Cholesterol 25

CHAPTER 4: LIFESTYLE TIPS FOR METABOLIC HEALTH 27

CHAPTER 5: ENERGIZING BREAKFASTS 33

    1. Blueberry Banana Smoothie 34

    2. Strawberry Almond Oats Smoothie 34

    3. Mixed Berries Smoothie Fusion 35

    4. Green Avocado Smoothie 35

    5. Creamy Spinach and Pear Smoothie 36

    6. Strawberry Smoothie Bowl with nuts and granola 36

    7. Quinoa High-Protein Breakfast Bowl 37

8. Overnight Chia seeds Breakfast Bowl ... 38

9. Oatmeal Breakfast Bowl ... 38

10. Scrambled Eggs and Veggie Breakfast Bowl ... 39

11. Hard Boiled Eggs Veggie Salad ... 40

12. Almond Yogurt Parfait With Assorted Fruits ... 40

13. Overnight Oatmeal High-Fiber Breakfast ... 41

14. Cinnamon Sweet Potato Oatmeal Pancakes ... 42

15. Muesli and Oatmeal Waffle With Apricots ... 43

CHAPTER 6: POWER LUNCHES ... 44

1. Sesame Chicken with Sauteed Veggies ... 45

2. Garlic Salmon Patties With Coleslaw Salad ... 45

3. Whole Wheat Tuna Wrap ... 46

4. Grilled Turkey And Veggie Wrap ... 47

5. Quinoa Black Bean Salad With Lime Dressing ... 47

6. Green Spinach Pasta With Creamy Parmesan Sauce ... 48

7. Peach And Avocado Salad With Feta Cheese Topping ... 48

8. Blueberry And Arugula Salad With Cheese ... 49

9. Crunchy Strawberry Spinach Salad ... 49

10. Mixed Beans And Veggie Salad ... 50

11. Edamame Beans Cucumber Kale Salad ... 50

12. Grilled Chicken Breast With Avocado And Pomegranate Seeds ... 51

13. Broccoli Veggie Pasta Salad With Pine Nuts ... 51

CHAPTER 7: DINNERS FOR SPEEDING UP YOUR METABOLISM ... 53

1. Greek Turkey Lettuce Rolls ... 54

2. Seared Scallops With Spinach ... 54

3. Chicken Zucchini Frittata Casserole ... 55

4. Grilled Mahi-Mahi With Mango Salsa ... 55

5. Slow-Cooked Lemon Basil Chicken ... 56

6. Slow-Cooked Chicken Fajitas ... 56

7. Eggplant And Chickpea Stew 57

8. Grilled Tofu And Quinoa Bowl 57

9. Moroccan Lamb With Cauliflower Rice 58

10. Slow-cooked barbecue Chicken 58

11. Avocado Tuna Salad 59

12. Turkey Meatballs With Zucchini Noodles 59

13. Herbed Chicken Thighs With Cauliflower Mash 60

CHAPTER 8: SNACKS FOR ENERGY 61

1. Homemade Flaxseed And Oats Energy-Rich Bars 62

2. Homemade Mixed Nuts And Muesli Energy Bites 62

3. Homemade Dates And Dried Cherries Energy Bars 63

4. Homemade Dates And Dried Fruits Energy Bars 63

5. Homemade Almond And Oats Energy Bars 64

6. Oats And Hemp Seeds Energy Bites 64

7. Oats And Peach Fusion Smoothie 65

8. Fiber-Rich Almond Chocolate Smoothie Bowl 66

9. Lime And Paprika-Seasoned Chickpeas 66

10. Almond Raspberry Smoothie 67

11. Banana Oatmeal Cookies 67

12. Quinoa And Chia Seeds Energy Bites With Berries 68

13. Healthy Fiber-Rich Fruits Salad Bowl 68

CHAPTER 9: DRINKS TO FUEL YOUR DAY 69

1. Golden Turmeric Cinnamon-Infused Milk 70

2. Lemon and Ginger-infused Tea 70

3. Lemon-infused Rosemary Tea 71

4. Mint-infused Fenugreek Seeds Tea 71

5. Orange-Infused Oolong Iced Tea 72

6. Lemon-infused Ginkgo Biloba Tea 72

7. Energy Blast Strawberry Drink 73

8. Mango Oats Smoothie 73

9. Pomegranate and Beet Drink 74

10. Refreshing Lime and Cherry Drink 74

11. Green Booster Energy Drink 75

12. Tropical Pineapple Energy Drink 75

13. Citrusy Peach Smoothie 76

CHAPTER 10: DETOX MEALS TO BOOST METABOLISM 77

1. Green Broccoli Salad With Olives And Lime Dressing 78

2. Spinach Arugula Pear Salad With Walnuts 78

3. Citrusy Detox Green Smoothie 79

4. Lime-Infused Chickpea Mint Avocado Bowl 79

5. Whole Wheat Quinoa Wrap With Asparagus And Beans 80

6. Green Detox Smoothie 80

7. Orange Arugula Pecan Salad With Balsamic Vinegar Dressing 81

8. Cauliflower Kale Chickpea Bowl With Parsley 81

9. Spinach Beet Quinoa Detox Salad 82

10. Zucchini Basil-Infused Soup 82

11. Cranberry Detox Mint Juice 83

12. Broccoli And Zucchini Salad with Olive Oil Dill Dressing 83

13. Blackberry Arugula Salad with Cashews 84

8-WEEK MEAL PLAN 85

GROCERY LIST 94

REFERENCES 116

RECIPE INDEX 117

INTRODUCTION

The Power of Metabolism: Fueling Limitless Health

Metabolism is one of the processes that can turn food into energy, which is essential in enabling life. It is one of the most elementary functions guaranteeing the optimization of all operations in the human body. It encloses a series of chemical reactions occurring in every body cell. The food we eat is transformed into molecules like glucose, fats, and proteins as energy sources that the cells use to perform various tasks like repairing tissues and maintaining organ function. This energy supervises blood circulation, thinking, sleeping, and other bodily functions.

The mechanism of metabolism is not limited to burning calories. In fact, it has several other roles in the body of a human being. It enables the regulation of body weight, control of hormonal secretions, absorption of key nutrients, and aids the contraction of muscles. It is accountable for delivering strength all over the body regarding physical power, mental health, and sharpening concentration.

A well-regulated metabolism is necessary for maintaining and fueling limitless health! It helps improve digestion and maintain steady energy levels in the body. Also, the power of metabolism expands even further since it plays a crucial role in disease prevention. It regulates cholesterol and maintains blood pressure for long-term health. A healthy metabolism can help prevent inflammation- the ultimate cause of many chronic conditions. Moreover, notorious diseases like obesity, diabetes, and other cardiovascular issues can be avoided by adopting a healthy lifestyle and determining metabolic efficiency. Food intake, water intake, and regular exercise are some factors that should be considered to boost a healthy metabolism. A healthy metabolism boosts the immune system and, therefore, enables your body to recover from any sickness or injury in a shorter period. Consequentially, without any doubt, metabolism is the key to boundless health!

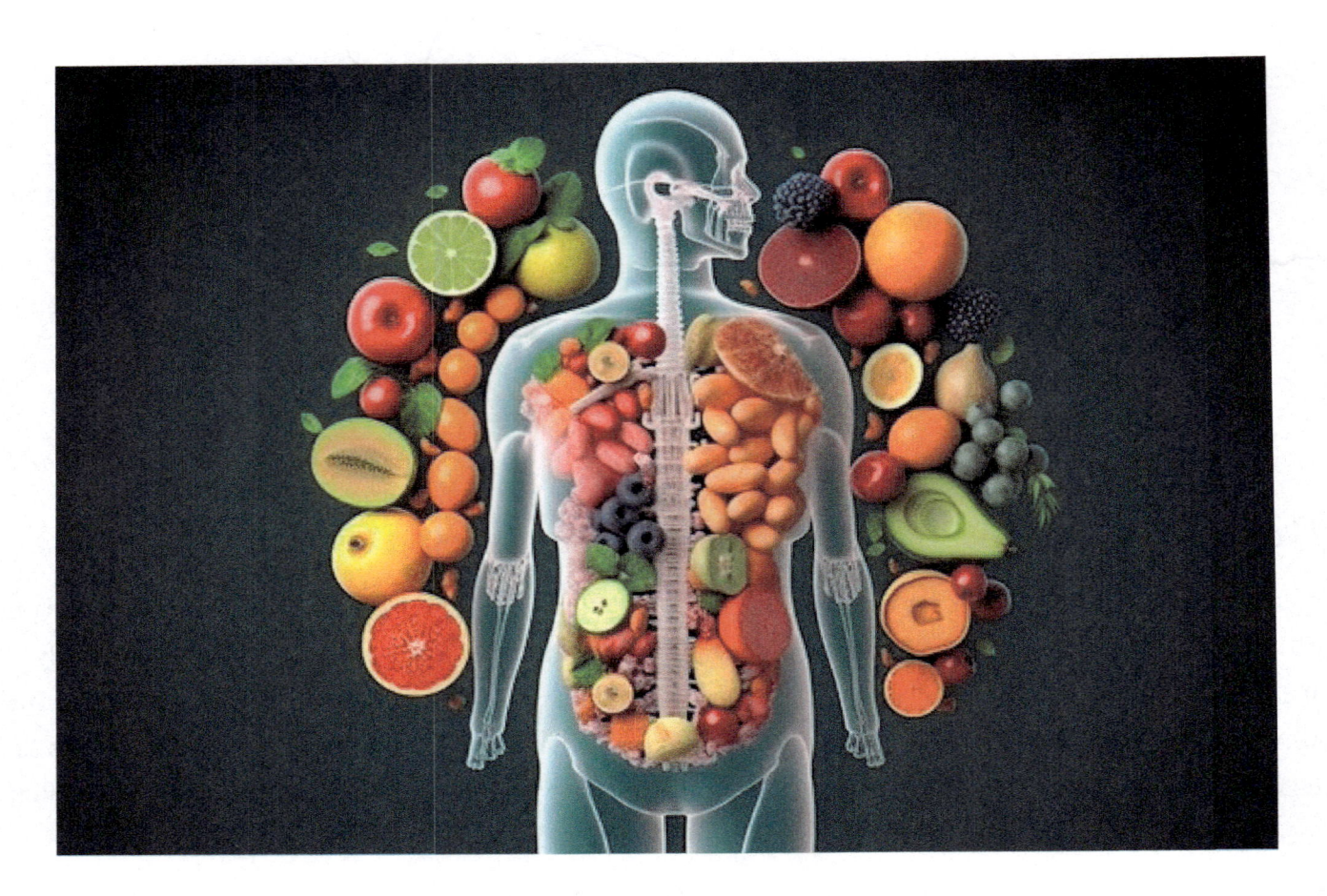

How Food Affects Energy and Well-Being

"You are what you eat" is not just a phrase but holds great significance in human lives. We work, play, study, and do every single activity based on the energy produced by the food we eat. The best treat a person can give themselves is eating and living healthier. The best possible food we can eat is the key to getting the most energy. Eating smaller portions of the least processed foods with high nutritional content and less fats is the ultimate way to go. While a cheeseburger with mayo dip sauce might be delicious, its nutritional value is unsatisfactory. Canned and packaged foods may have a longer shelf life and expiration date, but they are full of preservatives, trans fats, and artificial ingredients- all that your gut hates. Similarly, fatty foods are very tasty and comforting as we eat them, but they don't provide the body with the energy it needs. Instead, these foods, when eaten in higher amounts, make you lethargic.

As far as food is concerned, your food intake timing can also affect your energy levels. Not having enough breaks between meals or staying on an empty stomach for a long time are both unfavorable for your body and can be severe for your health. Laying down immediately after eating your meal is also an unhealthy approach, slowing digestion and causing heartburn.

So, the food, its quality, quantity, and way of consumption all affect a person's energy and well-being. Here are some tips to make food the best friend of your health and well-being:

- Choose seasonal products. Fruits and vegetables should be consumed in season to improve overall well-being.
- Red meat and fish, highly rich in Omega-3 fatty acids, are great sources of protein that help in improving overall health.
- Always select foods that contain complex carbohydrates so that your body can get all the key nutrients at the right time.
- Nuts and seeds should be consumed as snacks or added to smoothies and yogurt parfait mixed with fruits. Oats and chia seeds are rich in fiber and protein, essential for maintaining blood glucose levels and overall health.
- Foods rich in vitamins, folic acid, magnesium, and zinc help reduce fatigue.
- Stay away from mindless eating! If you are informed of what's on your plate, then you can maintain optimal health in the long run.
- Keeping an eye on your hydration is vital for human health. Although water doesn't provide energy in the form of calories, it facilitates the energetic processes in the body. So, it is high time you swapped your soft drinks and caffeine shots for a glass of water.
- Regular meals, exercise, good sleep, and water will surely increase your energy levels, and on the other hand, cutting down on caffeine intake will improve your overall well-being.

The Science of Good Energy: Metabolism Explained

Metabolism is the combination of all chemical reactions that take place in a living body necessary to sustain life. It is a biochemical process in which foods and their parts are broken down into simpler forms, and the elements or nutrients are then used by the cells to produce energy. The science of good energy can be understood by comprehending the two metabolic processes: catabolism and anabolism. If metabolic functions happen efficiently in our body, we grow positively, our tissues are repaired, and our maintenance and health are assured.

The food we eat has a great influence on the rate of metabolism taking place in the body. Some nutrients, however, affect metabolism differently than other nutrients. For example, proteins have a higher "**THERMIC EFFECT**" than fats or carbohydrates because our body needs more energy to digest proteins. Following a balanced diet, especially by eating meals rich in protein, whole grain foods, fruits, and vegetables, can help maintain a healthy metabolism.

What You'll Find in This Cookbook

This cookbook will be your favorite read, especially if you're concerned about giving your body the gift of good energy and metabolic upgrade. We all have a fitness freak inside us, and so this book will absolutely catch your attention. This book contains everything about learning metabolism and all of its aspects. Once you get into it, you'll realize this cookbook is an easy and handy piece of information on how anabolic and catabolic processes take place in your body and how you can learn about your specific metabolic type. With such fantastic knowledge right on your bookshelf, you can easily set your dietary and other routines in a way as to maintain the optimal rate of your metabolism.

The answer to what makes this cookbook special lies in its easy and simple language, used for everyone to understand the depths of metabolism easily. Here is a series of summarized points that explain "What you will find in this cookbook"!

- What Metabolism is- this cookbook defines metabolism in a way that is easy to grasp and remember forever.

- Here, you will discover what types of metabolism exist, as well as brief descriptions of each common kind. This book will teach you more about the right dietary preferences in relation to each of the metabolism types. Hence, you can easily incorporate a diet routine that will enhance your body's metabolism.

- In this book, you will not only learn about metabolism, but also about what metabolism is not! For ages, people have tried to explain metabolism in their own terms, which gave rise to many myths surrounding metabolic systems. An effort has been made to debunk some of these myths to really understand metabolism.

- This cookbook will educate you on how hormones regulate the metabolic processes in your body. Once you learn metabolism on this level, boosting your metabolism while checking and maintaining optimum hormone levels will seem super easy.

- In this book, you will also learn what superfoods are as well as the superfoods that will enhance your metabolism rate. You will find out about LDL cholesterol, and also about those diets that help to keep bad cholesterol in optimum ranges.

- Finally, you will discover some great recipes to prepare healthy foods that do not take much time to prepare and can be easily included in one's daily diet plan. With these recipes, it will be possible to maintain a healthy metabolic system.

CHAPTER 1:
UNDERSTANDING METABOLISM

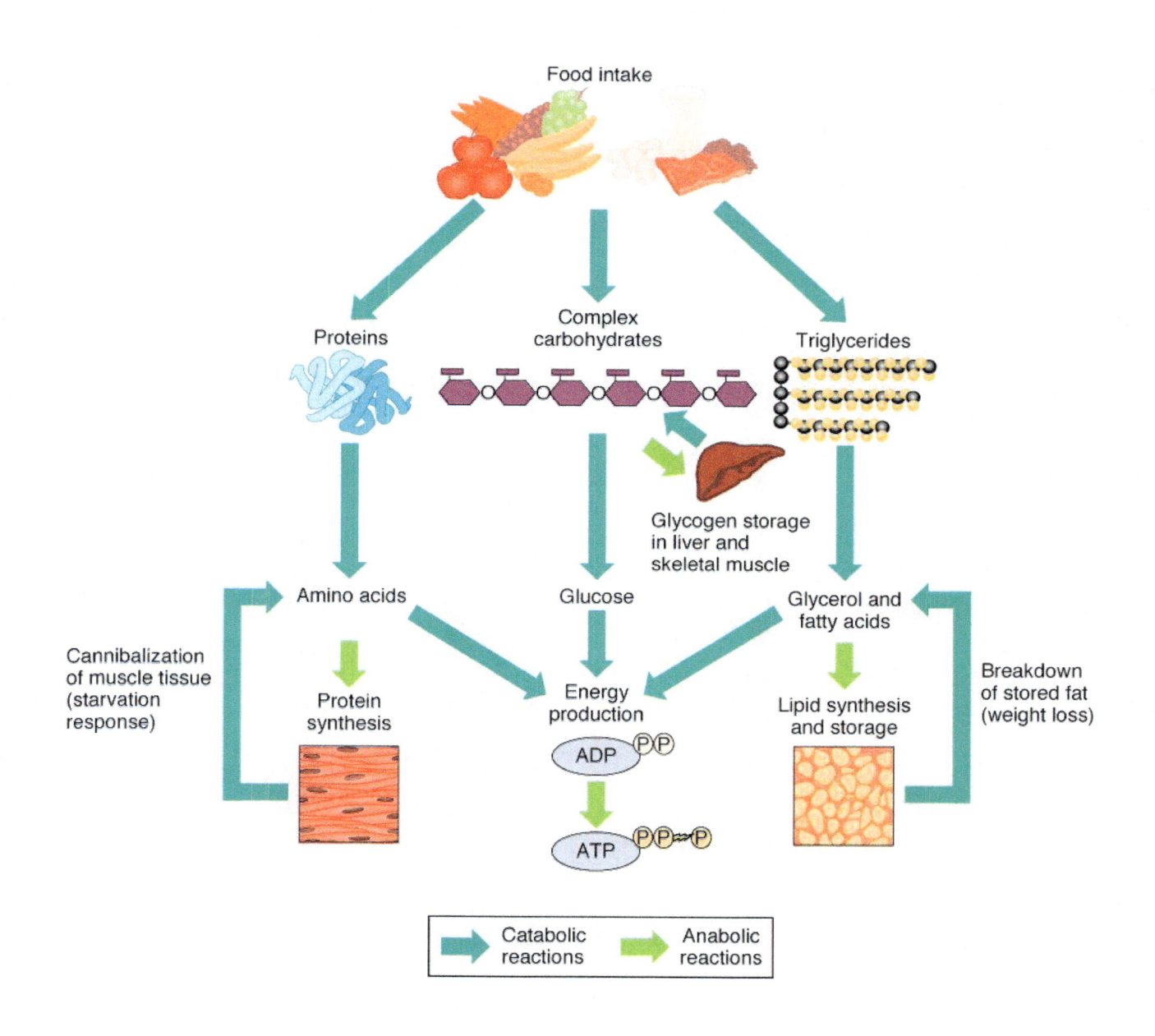

What Is Metabolism?

The term metabolism has its roots in the Greek words "meta," which means transcending, and "bole," meaning change or transformation. Metabolism is a very complex, vast, and miraculous process of biochemical reactions that occur within all living organisms, including Homo sapiens (human beings), in order to maintain and process the biochemistry and physical aspects of life. It involves the breakdown and synthesis of organic molecules, energy production, and waste elimination.

There are two essential processes regarding metabolism:

- Catabolism
- Anabolism

Catabolism is defined as the process during which complex molecules are broken down into simpler molecules, and energy is released in the form of ATP. The simplest examples in this category are the digestion of food and the process of breaking glycogen into glucose for energy.

On the other hand, **anabolism** comprises the build-up of complex molecules from simpler molecules, during which process energy is required. For example, the build-up of muscle tissue from amino acids falls in the category of the anabolic process.

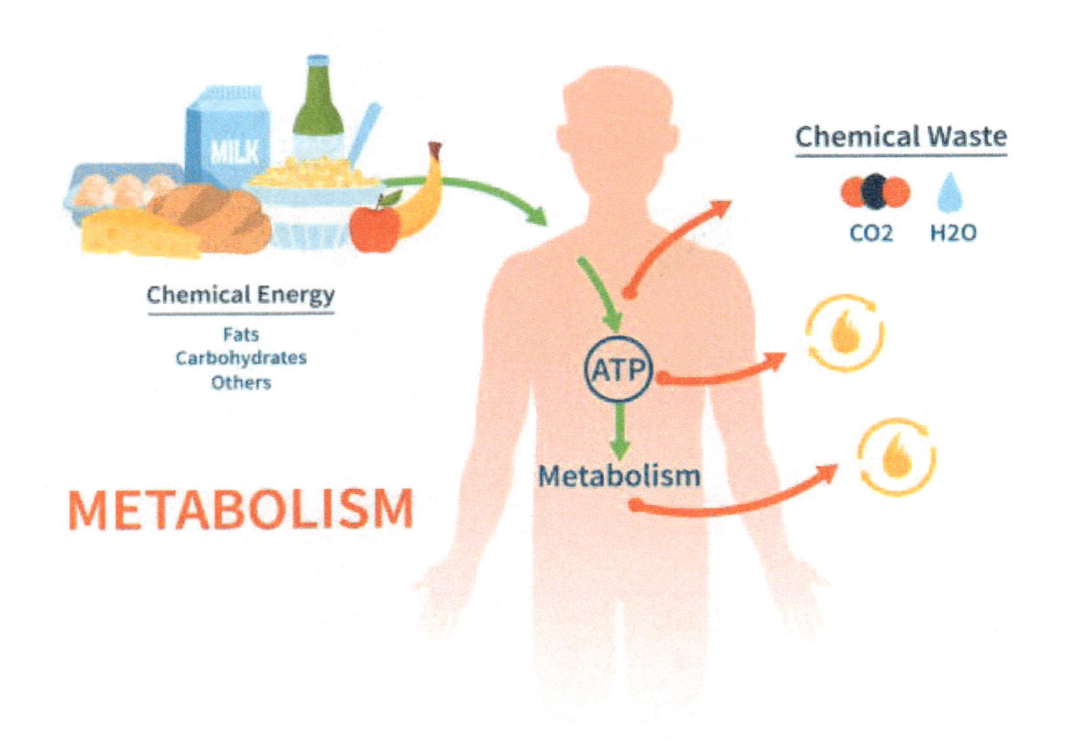

Metabolic Types: How Your Body Processes Energy

Knowledge of the human mechanisms for the utilization of energy is essential for understanding the complex issue of metabolism. For instance, the use of oxygen is classified as aerobic or anaerobic, and the types of nutrients used include carbohydrates, proteins, or fats. In addition, metabolism can also be categorized based on the energy requirements of the organism, such as basal metabolic rate (BMR), resting metabolic rate, and the thermic effect of food.

There are three main metabolic types. These are: fast oxidizers, slow oxidizers, and mixed oxidizers.

Fast Oxidizers: These people burn carbohydrates very fast and, therefore, feel hungry and tired due to the fluctuating blood sugar levels. For continuous energy, they should concentrate on proteins and fats such as fish, rich in fatty acids, avocadoes, and nuts; they should avoid carbs. Consuming complex carbohydrates, such as sweet potatoes, instead of simple forms of carbohydrates prevents energy draining.

Slow Oxidizers: Slow oxidizers digest meals slowly and feel full for longer. They benefit from carb-rich diets since the body is dependent on carbohydrates to produce energy. They need fruits, vegetables, and whole grain products and should consider lighter fats, such as olive oil and lean meats. Eating high-fat meals makes people feel lethargic, so small portions of high-fat food on the plate are encouraged.

Mixed Oxidizers: Mixed Oxidizers are a blend of both categories, capable of metabolizing carbohydrates, fats, and proteins effectively. They are best served by a diet which includes equal portions of carbohydrates, proteins, and fats.

Common Myths About Metabolism

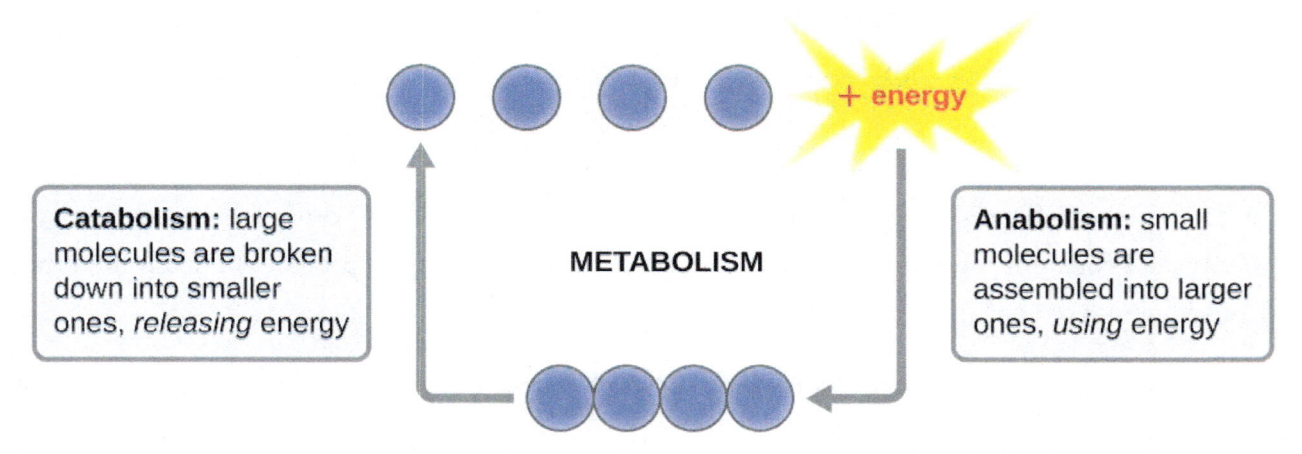

Catabolism: large molecules are broken down into smaller ones, *releasing* energy

METABOLISM

Anabolism: small molecules are assembled into larger ones, *using* energy

+ energy

Metabolism is a complex process. While the above terms help to make the concept easy to understand, this bodily process is more than just burning calories. Metabolism is associated with losing weight, and all for the right reasons. However, this is not the only factor in determining the QOL and healthy weight management. There are many myths associated with metabolism. And with these myths, all sorts of beliefs about metabolism ensue. People have wrong perceptions about metabolism, which can make them embrace various quick fixes, fad diets, or unnecessary lifestyle changes that may have nothing to do with metabolism.

Let's try to discover and then debunk some of the most common myths circulating about metabolism.

1. **Thin people are fast oxidizers!** This is the most common and widely believed misconception about metabolism. Metabolism is the burning of calories to sustain a daily lifestyle. It's about the energy our body uses at rest, known as BMR- Basal Metabolic Rate. Hence, thinner people have a lower BMR than heavier or larger individuals because they need fewer calories to meet their daily energy requirements. So, while their thinness can be associated with their metabolism, other factors like genetics, their daily dietary routine, and their activity levels are some other significant factors affecting their thinness and lower body weight.

2. **Don't eat before bed- it will turn to fat!** We're told not to eat before bedtime to ensure better digestion and avoid bloating and gas issues, so believing that snacks would be turned into fat is a rather funny myth! We might all have heard once in our lifetime that what we eat just before bed is usually turned into fat. Our body is programmed very smartly, and metabolism doesn't work that way. Metabolism has little to do with the timing of eating and more to do with what we eat! Whether it is before bedtime or craving an afternoon/evening snack, make sure to make healthier choices and keep your portions in control. Some nuts, fruits, low-fat yogurt, etc., are some options to consider if you have a nighttime craving.

3. **Those with a fast metabolism can eat anything!** Another widespread misconception about metabolism is that those with a fast metabolism can eat as much as they want and not gain weight. Indeed, some people have a faster metabolism; they burn more calories even when they are at rest, but no one can continue to eat junk food without consequences forever. Thus, a fast metabolism should not mean one can indulge in unlimited unhealthy and junk foods. Because in the end, even if your higher metabolic rate doesn't convert you into a fat person, still the larger amount of unhealthy foods will ultimately affect your health in negative aspects. One can get high cholesterol levels, diabetes, or other cardiovascular problems without being overweight just because of constant junk food eating. So, metabolism is not going to protect you from the unwanted consequences of your improper diet.

4. **Metabolism means burning calories!** People consider metabolism only as the breaking down of food and burning of calories. This is true for sure, but not the complete truth. Metabolism consists of two processes: anabolism and catabolism. Catabolism is all about breaking down, but anabolism is about building compounds using energy, like carbohydrates, in the form of glycogen and building fats for storage purposes. Both processes combine to create a proper metabolism, so only breaking down things and burning isn't the whole definition of metabolism.

5. **Our metabolic rates are genetically determined and stay constant!** Metabolism has much to do with our genes. However, a widely believed myth is that our metabolic rates are final by birth. Metabolic rates don't need to stay constant. We can boost our BMR by strength training! Muscles increase metabolism. So, if we adopt an active lifestyle and concentrate on building our lean muscle mass, we can increase our metabolism rates.

Role of Hormones In Metabolism

The metabolism process efficiently converts our food into the energy that our body needs for daily activities. This series of chemical reactions also helps to repair tissues and build storage compounds in our body. This complex process doesn't happen in our body on its own- some important hormones regulate the proper functioning of metabolism. Hormones signal our body organs and guide them on how best to utilize the energy in the body. The hormones' role in metabolism is important as fluctuations in their levels can greatly affect this process in the long run. The disruption of hormones can contribute to the development of obesity, diabetes, and thyroid diseases. Some of these hormones are discussed below for a proper understanding of how they affect our metabolism.

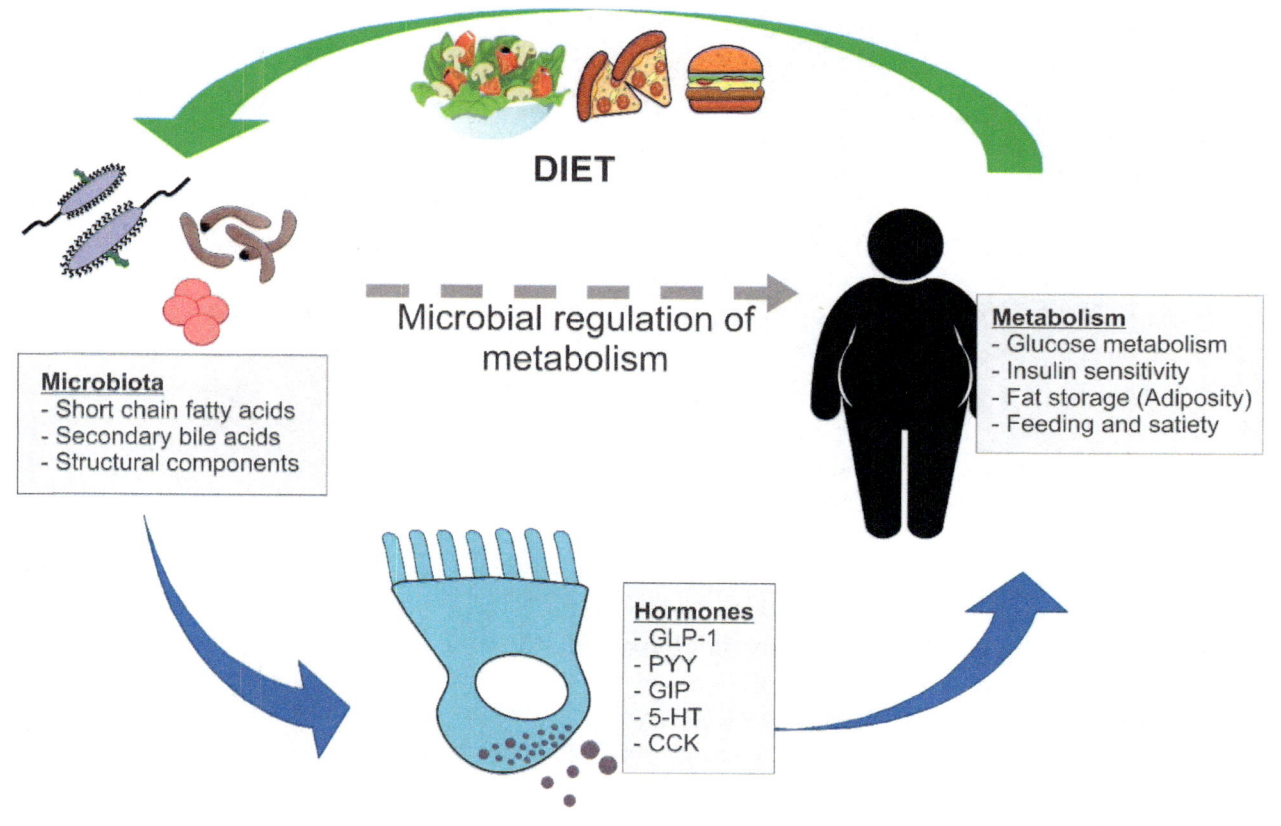

Insulin

Insulin is well known as the sugar-controlling hormone. This hormone is very important in regulating carbohydrate metabolism as well. It is secreted by the pancreatic cells and regulates the distribution of glucose in the entire body and its transportation in the bloodstream. As soon as carbs enter our body and cause a rise in blood sugar, insulin comes to the rescue! It transfers glucose toward cells for either usage or storage as a future energy reserve. It also aids in the metabolism of excess glucose to glycogen stored in the liver and reduces lipolysis, thus ensuring that glucose is utilized as the primary energy source.

Any disruption of insulin regulation causes a state of chaos in the body, leading to metabolic disorders like diabetes type 1 and type 2. If diabetes is not properly managed, it can cause a lot of damage to your body organs, nerves, and blood vessels, even proving to be fatal in some cases.

IMPORTANCE OF INSULIN

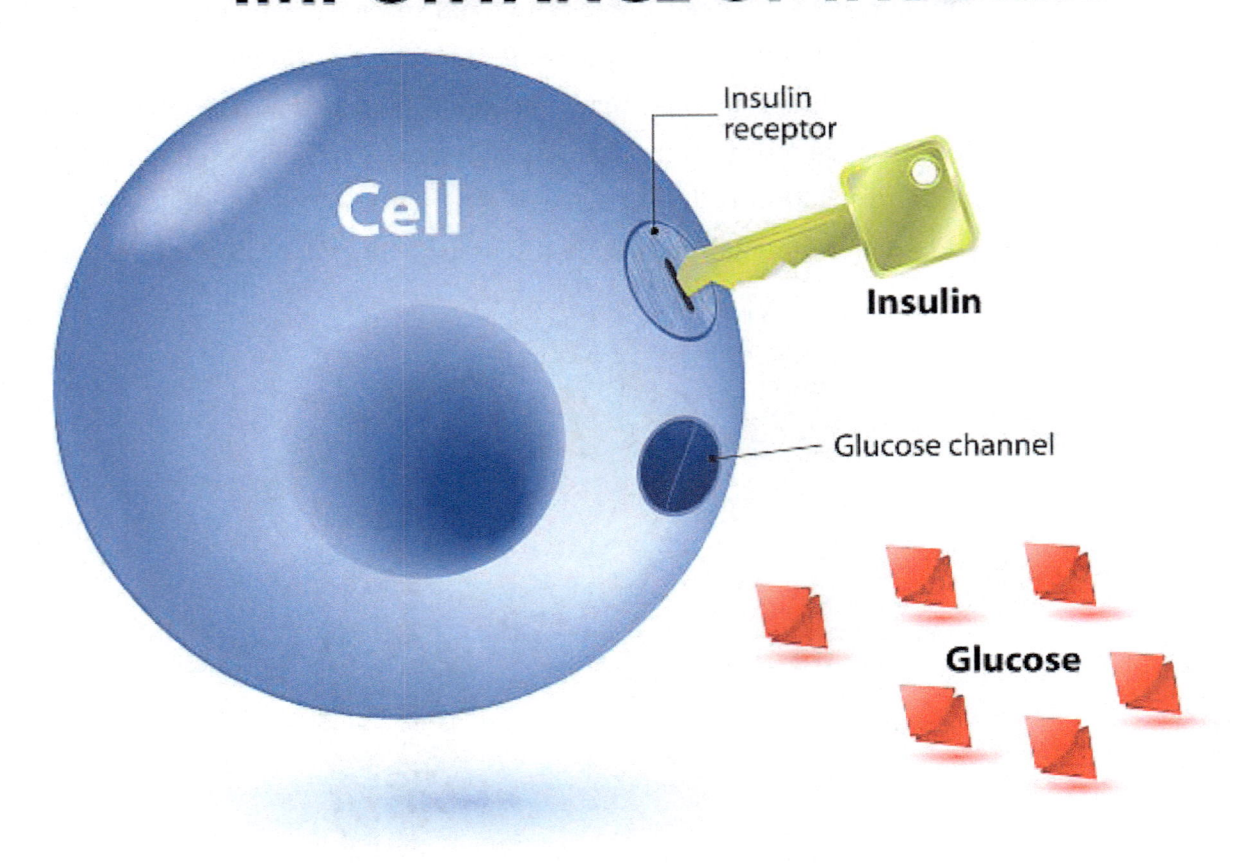

Thyroid Hormones

There are three thyroid hormones released by the thyroid gland:

- Triiodothyronine (T3)
- Tetra-iodothyronine (T4), also called as Thyroxine
- Calcitonin

All these hormones, particularly T4 and T3, play a significant role in controlling the basal metabolic rates of our body. Calling these hormones the master regulators of metabolism won't be an exaggeration. They are the primary hormones that govern metabolic speeds. They are involved in regulating all physiological factors of the body, including heart rate, body temperature, growth, and even development.

When the amounts of thyroid hormones are low, hypothyroidism occurs. It is a condition in which the metabolic reactions are reduced, and the symptoms may include a swollen face, weight gain, fatigue, and hypersensitivity to cold. On the other hand, hyperthyroidism, which involves excessive production of thyroid hormones, increases metabolism associated with weight loss, increased pulse rate, and nervousness.

THYROID HORMONES

TRH - Thyroid Releasing Hormone
TSH - Thyroid Stimulating Hormone
T$_3$ - Triiodothyronine hormone
T$_4$ - Thyroxine hormone

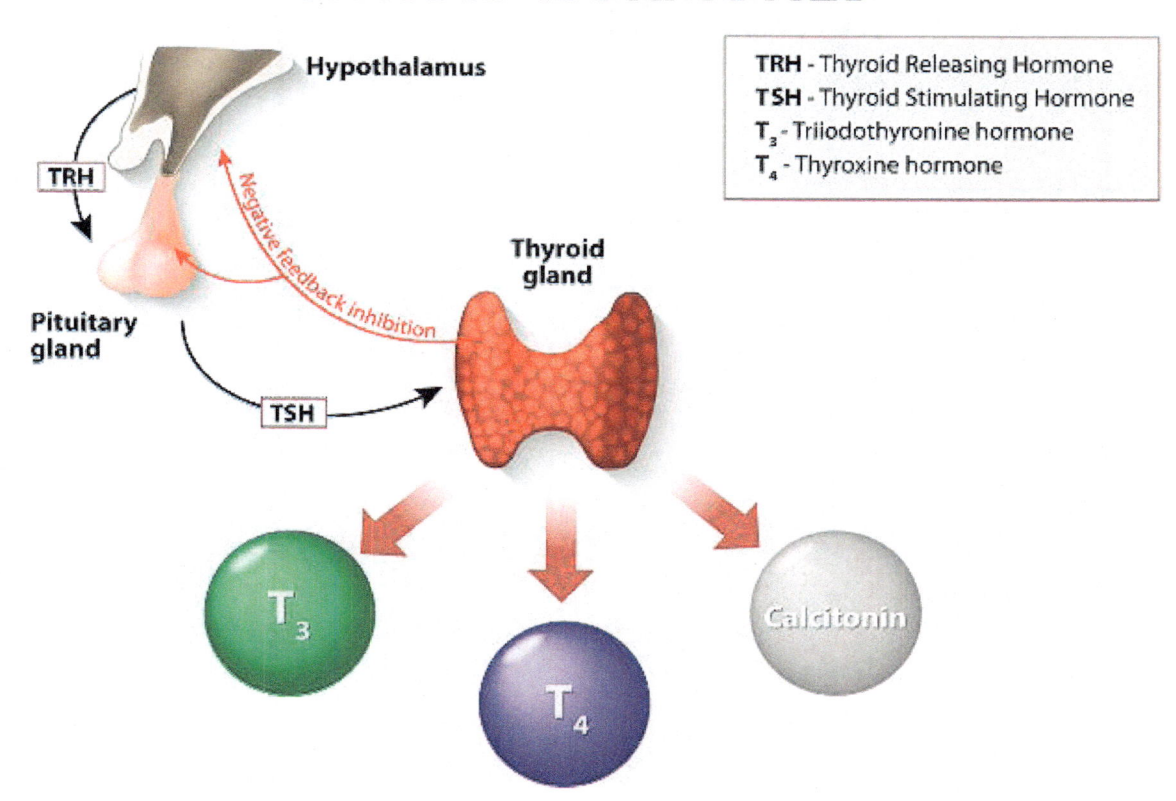

Sex Hormones

You might have heard or seen that as soon as a woman hits menopause, she gets stubborn fat around her belly. This is because of estrogens. Estrogens regulate lipid metabolism and storage in women by storing more fat in the hips and thigh regions. However, as the rates of estrogens decrease in older ages, the fat is stored in the abdominal area of women. This can lead to obesity and increase the risk of cardiovascular diseases.

Testosterone, the sex hormone of males, works by anabolic pathways, building muscle mass in the body. It boosts the metabolism. Hence, when men turn older, their testosterone levels decline, their accumulation of fat increases, and muscle mass decreases, resulting in a decreased rate of metabolism.

Cortisol

Cortisol is the stress hormone as it responds when the body faces any fasting or stressful condition. It affects the metabolism according to stress levels in our body. When stress levels increase, cortisol increases glucose production. It metabolizes non-carbohydrate sources and transforms them into glucose to ensure a constant supply of energy to the body under pressure. Hence, chronic stress has been shown to cause weight gain and metabolic syndrome.

Thus, it can be stated that to achieve and sustain metabolic health, the hormones should be well regulated, which requires adherence to proper diet and meal planning, regular exercise, stress reduction, and hormone therapy if necessary.

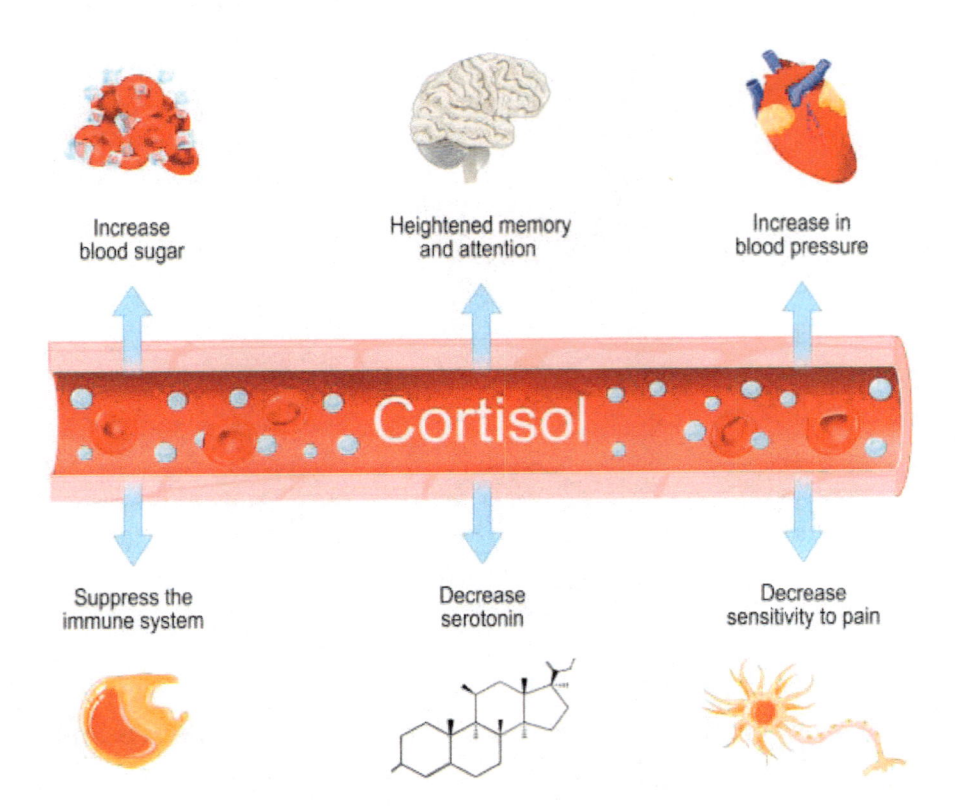

CHAPTER 2:
SUPERFOODS FOR METABOLISM

What Are Superfoods? And Why Do They Matter For Metabolism?

Superfoods are the foods that are claimed to have extra health benefits. They are highly nutritious and can often be linked to the prevention or treatment of certain diseases. These nutrient-dense foods are considered extremely healthy because they contain many vitamins and minerals. Some popular superfoods include berries, green leafy vegetables, nuts, seeds, and fatty fish, such as salmon. It is important to note that the term 'superfoods' is not a scientific definition of a specific food type; rather, it is a marketing term to emphasize the nutrient density of certain foods.

Superfoods are very nourishing and contain a large amount of carbohydrates, proteins, and fats. Hence, they increase the rate of metabolism. Such superfoods keep your cravings at bay by requiring more energy from the body to digest them. In this way, you feel fuller and satiated for longer. It is an easy and healthy way to cut down excess sugar and salt intake.

Top Superfoods For Metabolism

Here's a list of top Superfoods that are beneficial for metabolic support and contribute to better health & well-being.

1) **Berries:** One of the key superfoods for metabolism is berries. Berries, such as blueberries, strawberries, blackberries, and raspberries, being antioxidant-rich, are highly loaded with vitamins and fiber. Berries play an essential role in regulating blood sugar levels and help to lower cravings. That's why they are a great option for boosting metabolic health.

2) **Leafy Greens:** Another important addition required for boosting metabolic health is leafy greens, especially spinach. Spinach is low in calories and rich in nutrients. Being rich in iron, spinach plays a key role in transporting oxygen to the blood and supporting energy metabolism.

3) **Chia Seeds:** Chia seeds are a rich source of omega-3 fatty acids, which boost eye and brain health, along with fighting inflammation. They also contain fiber, which helps in promoting gut health. The high protein content of chia seeds makes them an ideal choice for those who are trying to lose weight.

4) **Avocados:** The unique trait that makes avocados a superfood for metabolism is their high content of monounsaturated fats. Due to the presence of healthy fats, avocados aid in increasing the absorption of vitamins, regulating hormones, improving digestive health, and sustaining cholesterol levels in the normal range.

5) **Quinoa: When it comes to the superfood that is best for metabolism, quinoa comes at the top!** Undoubtedly, quinoa is considered a great superfood for boosting metabolism. Quinoa is a complete protein package! Being rich in fiber, it keeps you full for a longer period and maintains your gut health.

6) **Almonds:** Almonds are a great source of healthy fats, fiber, and protein. Consumption of almonds helps to regulate blood glucose levels, lower cravings, boost brain health, and control your appetite. Enjoy almonds by adding them to smoothies and yogurt parfaits!

7) **Green Tea:** Due to the presence of catechins, green tea is considered the best food to increase metabolic rate and improve the process of fat oxidation. Consumption of one cup of green tea daily helps in weight management and improves overall well-being.

8) **Greek Yogurt:** Greek yogurt is rich in proteins, probiotics, and calcium. The protein content in Greek yogurt is directly proportional to the thermic effect of food, which means that your body is burning more calories during digestion, thus aiding in weight loss.

9) **Oats:** A soluble fiber, beta-glucan, makes them an excellent choice for boosting metabolic health. It is safe to say that regular consumption of oatmeal provides a quick energy boost to the body. They help regulate blood glucose levels, increase the feeling of fullness and lower cholesterol levels.

10) **Coconut oil**: Coconut oil is highly rich in medium-chain triglycerides. It increases energy expenditure and boosts the process of fat burning. Its unique feature is that it breaks down in a different way as compared to other fats, so it is truly a must-have addition to a metabolism-boosting diet.

Incorporating Superfoods in Daily Life

Adding superfoods to your everyday meals can be a game changer. Incorporating them will not only provide you with a healthy and nutritious diet but will also add variety and deliciousness to your dining table.

They say breakfast is the most important meal of the day! You can incorporate superfoods into your breakfast, starting your day fresh and energetic. Add berries, chia seeds, or spinach to your smoothies. Mix nuts, seeds, or a spoonful of chia seeds into your oatmeal, and prepare for a productive day!

Incorporating superfoods into your lunch and dinner gives you a feeling of satiety and keeps your body functions under check. You can add them to your salads, wraps, and even soups. Aim to include at least 1 or 2 superfoods in every meal and make it a habit!

Superfoods act as a better substitute for junk food. They not only provide you with sustainable long-term energy but are also low in calories. Junk food, on the other hand, is a poor source of vitamins, proteins, and healthy fat. They only provide short-term energy, cover much of the daily caloric intake, and make you feel hungry soon after.

So, the next time you feel a little hungry and want to snack, have a handful of nuts , some berries or an avocado and see the change for yourself!

CHAPTER 3:
LOWERING LDL CHOLESTEROL

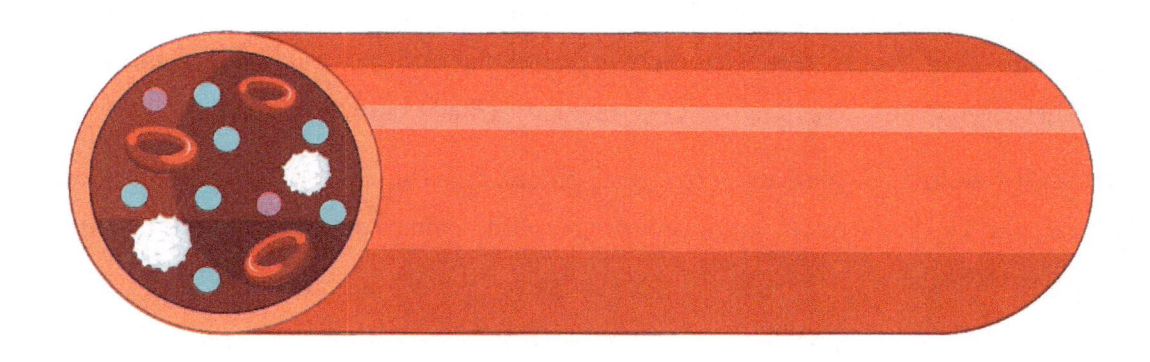

GOOD CHOLESTEROL

BAD CHOLESTEROL

Understanding LDL Cholesterol & Its Impact On Health

The human body is a complex, intricate, and yet fascinating system involving various biochemical and hormonal processes. Our behaviors, diets, routines, stress levels, and various other factors directly influence our metabolism. Fat, in the form of triglycerides and cholesterol, acts as a precursor to form Lipoproteins, namely High-Density Lipoproteins (HDL), Low-density Lipoproteins (LDL) & Very Low-Density Lipoproteins (VLDL).

Low-Density Lipoprotein (LDL) is a cholesterol-rich lipoprotein derived from its precursor, VLDL. After its formation in the liver, VLDL loses triglycerides in the tissues, successively forming intermediate-density lipoprotein (IDH). IDH adds cholesterol and transforms it into LDL.

LDL is the lipoprotein responsible for the transport of circulating cholesterol to the tissues. The tissues require cholesterol to maintain cell membrane integrity, hormone production, and other important processes.

LDL is composed of 8-10% cholesterol, 20-28% Phospholipids, 10-15% TAG, 5-10% Apolipoprotein, and 37-48% cholesterol esters. LDL clings to cell surface receptors via Apo-B100, which then transports cholesterol to the cells.

While LDL under normal levels is essential for cell membrane, hormone synthesis, vitamin D, and bile acid production, its increased levels are extremely dangerous, and pose a health hazard, especially for cardiovascular diseases. That's why LDL has been labeled as 'bad cholesterol.'

Increased LDL is the leading cause of atherosclerotic plaque disease. Excess LDL infiltrates the arterial walls, where it gets oxidized. The subsequent inflammatory response causes plaque formation, leading to hardening and narrowing of arteries.

Increased levels of LDL also have a direct association with cardiovascular diseases. The deposition of LDL cholesterol on the arterial walls of the heart or brain can lead to heart attack or stroke. Suppose the coronary artery, which supplies blood to the heart, is affected by atherosclerosis. In that case, it will lead to coronary artery disease (CAD) with frequent chest pain (angina) and a high risk of heart failure.

High levels of LDL are also linked with Peripheral Artery Disease (PAD) and thrombus formation.

Before discussing the foods that lower LDL, let's discuss the various risk factors that can increase LDL.

- A diet high in cholesterol and trans fat, such as full-fat dairy products, junk food, etc.
- Lack of physical activity decreases good cholesterol (HDL) and increases LDL.
- Inherited diseases, such as familial hypercholesterolemia.
- Obesity, smoking, and diabetes are also some of the major risk factors.

Foods & Nutrients That Lower LDL Cholesterol

Here's a list of foods and nutrients that lower LDL cholesterol.

- **Oatmeal**: Oatmeal is a healthy, fiber-rich start to your day. Oats' soluble fiber helps reduce LDL cholesterol absorption, supporting healthier levels.

- **Whole Grains**: Whole grains contain beta-glucan, which reduces LDL cholesterol by binding bile acids and promoting excretion.

- **Beans and Legumes:** Beans, lentils, and legumes in general contain soluble fiber, which aids in lowering LDL cholesterol through reduced absorption.

- **Nuts:** Almonds and walnuts are a good source of monounsaturated fats, polyunsaturated fats and plant sterols that lower LDL levels and support heart health.

- **Fatty Fish**: Omega-3-rich fatty fish, like salmon and mackerel, lower LDL cholesterol, and promote the increase of the levels of HDL, the 'good cholesterol'.

- **Olive Oil:** Olive oil is a heart-healthy choice, containing monounsaturated fats, which lower LDL and support HDL cholesterol.

- **Soy Products:** Soy-based products, such as tofu or soy milk, lower LDL levels owing to the presence of **soy protein.** Soy protein retards the production of cholesterol in the liver, leading to decreased LDL cholesterol levels.

- **Fruits:** Fruits, especially apples, grapes, and berries can help to promote cardiovascular health by keeping the LDL levels in check. These fruits are rich in soluble fiber, which binds cholesterol in the gastrointestinal tract and maintains LDL cholesterol.

- **Green Tea and Dark chocolate:** Green tea consists of an active ingredient named catechin. Catechin is a strong antioxidant. It acts based on a dual mechanism. It inhibits cholesterol absorption and retards its production in the liver. Except for green tea, moderate consumption of dark chocolate also improves cardiovascular health. It contains catechins and theobromine, which lower LDL levels and improve endothelial and cardiovascular functions.

Garlic: Garlic is one of the most important superfoods, ensuring cardiovascular health, boosting the immune system, and providing anti-inflammatory effects. Its role in maintaining LDL cholesterol is linked to its active ingredient, named allicin. Alicen increases the breakdown of LDL cholesterol and decreases the production of cholesterol in the liver. Increased breakdown and decreased production help to regulate the levels of LDL cholesterol.

CHAPTER 4:
LIFESTYLE TIPS FOR METABOLIC HEALTH

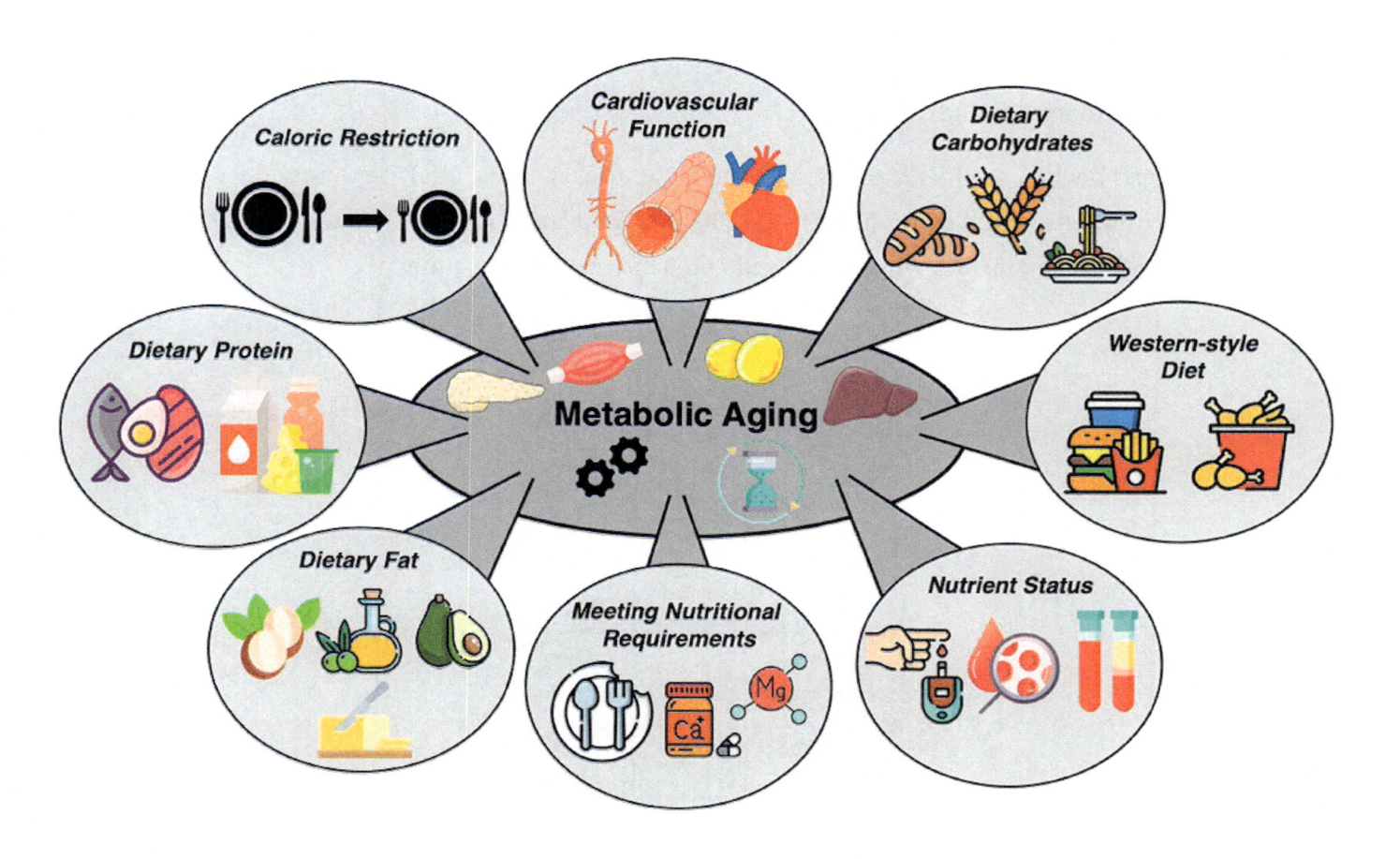

Now, as we have understood good energy, it's clear that when our metabolic health is cared for, our body utilizes nutrients and regulates energy balance efficiently. By regulating our metabolic health, we attract good energy for our day, and our energy levels remain steady throughout. This way, we get to have a nice stamina, and with the long-term regulation of metabolic health, we drag away the risk of so many metabolic and chronic diseases.

With these mentioned advantages, we understand that it is essential to keep our metabolic health in check not for a day or two but rather all along. That's where the routine modifications come. Once you follow a metabolic-friendly routine, the steady energy and positive changes you'll feel with it will be addictive. A good metabolism will really become your lifestyle.

Many factors are worthy to be considered when you decide to stick to good energy forever. Let's dive into them one by one:

A Balanced Diet: (of course!)

A balanced diet really just consists of proteins, carbs, and fats, all in recommended amounts. Proteins help to maintain your metabolic activity and health by helping you burn more calories while preserving your muscles.

Similarly, the right carbohydrates, like the complex ones and whole grains, help to enhance good energy in your body without causing a rise in blood sugar, hence preventing diabetes. Fruits and veggies, especially greens, are other metabolic-friendly choices.

As for fats, nuts and healthy seeds (flaxseeds, chia seeds, sunflower seeds, etc.) are the energy sources that aid in metabolism without disrupting your heart health. Fish, olive oil, and foods that contain omega-3 fatty acids are some other options to consider when you decide on which fats to consume.

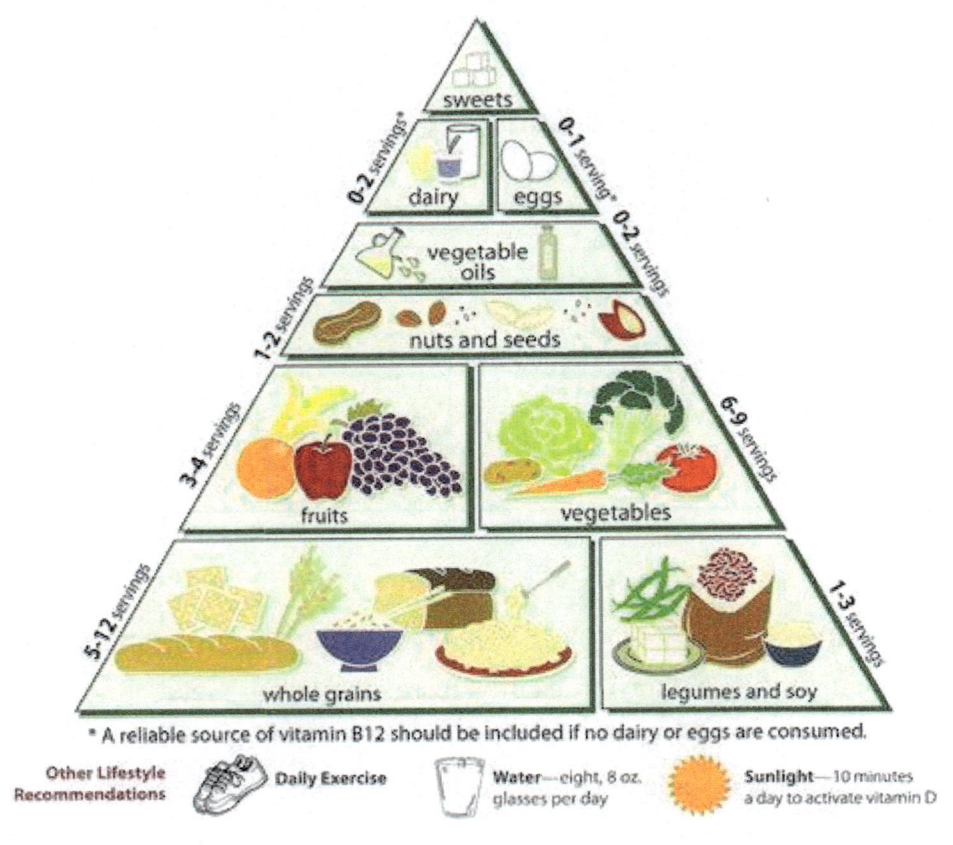

Nutrition Timing for Metabolic Health:

This might sound like a myth. However, several researches have shown the link between meal timing and metabolic health. They say, "Listen to and trust your body," and they are right. Being punctual with your body's clock is the way to go. There are many ways in which nutrition timing affects our metabolic health, and to maintain a healthy metabolism, it is essential to adopt nutrition timing as your lifestyle changes to maximize metabolic efficiency and advantages. Let's take a look at some of these points:

Circadian Rhythms: You can really achieve your metabolism-enhancing goals by eating according to your body's circadian clock. Diet studies have shown that it would be advantageous to consume food during the day. It is because the body is more metabolically active throughout the day, it has a better glucose tolerance, and thus it improves insulin sensitivity.

Fasting and Autophagy: There are many opinions about intermittent fasting. But one thing is true. Eating during a limited window and fasting the whole other day helps you get rid of dead cells in your body! Yes, this process is called autophagy. Autophagy happens when your body is in a fasting condition for a certain period and, hence, is deprived of nutrients. So, the catabolic processes are activated, and your body starts recycling its own cells for energy purposes, thus getting your damaged cells and proteins removed from your body.

Insulin Sensitivity: Eating regularly without skipping meals helps your body adapt to a consistent eating schedule and lowers the risk of insulin sensitivity.

Hormone Regulation: Did you know? Meal timings can influence hormonal production! Again, this can sound naïve; however, our circadian rhythms are strong and have a lot of effects on metabolic processes happening in our body. Insulin, cortisol, and growth hormone are some of the metabolic hormones impacted by our meal timing.

Digestion and Gut Health: Allowing for proper digestion time and eating in a relaxed state can aid in digestion and absorption of nutrients as well as in maintaining overall gut health. These processes help to maintain a healthy metabolism.

Boosting Metabolism: Eating protein-rich meals, especially in the morning, can kick-start your metabolism, while incorporating healthy fats and complex carbohydrates can sustain energy and support metabolic function.

Avoiding Late-Night Eating: Our body is sensitive to our natural biological clock. As we are more metabolically active during the day, it's just right to avoid binge eating or mindless eating late at night. Eating at times that are against our body's efficiency will, in turn, disrupt our metabolic health.

Listening to Hunger Cues: Following a healthy diet does not mean cutting off on essential food groups or giving up on your favorite cravings. One needs to keep their food portions in control. Listen to your body and eat according to your hunger and metabolic needs. Try to avoid overeating. Eating according to your hunger cues helps to maintain good energy in your body.

Consistency: We all know consistency is key! Good energy and maximum efficiency will become an essential part of your life only if you stick to your good dietary habits. Maintaining a regular pattern of eating can improve overall metabolic health.

Individual Variability: In the end, here it needs to be mentioned yet again that every person may have a different experience regarding the timing of meals with respect to all above mentioned factors, and that may be why everyone needs to try out and find what is the most effective and suitable for them.

Hydration:

Our body does not need energy only in the form of food; water and hydration are two other very important factors to maintain our overall health. A lot of biochemical processes happening inside our body need water electrolytes to function. Taking care of your hydration really means taking care of your metabolic health. If we drink the optimum quantity of water, our metabolic rates will be enhanced, which in turn proves that even a slight decrease in our hydration levels will reduce the rate of our metabolism. Staying hydrated helps you get rid of toxins inside your body and burn more calories than usual.

Physical Activity:

The more we work out, the more calories we burn, and thus the better is our metabolic health. With this being said, physical activity and exercise are crucial to maintaining a healthy metabolism and good energy. Exercise helps to increase your metabolic rate even when you are in a resting position. This really means that you are burning calories while doing simply nothing!

Some important types of exercising that can be your go-to to achieve your metabolic goals include:

- Weight lifting: Strength training helps to build muscle and enhance your metabolism. Strength training is a high-intensity type of exercise that boosts your BMR and increases the rate of your metabolic health.

- Cardio: These include swimming, brisk walking, cycling, running, etc., and they are named so for the right reasons; they improve your cardiac health. When our heart pumps right, our metabolism works fast and right, too.

- NEAT: It stands for "Non-Exercise Activity Thermogenesis." This might be your favorite. NEAT refers to the daily activities we all do that are not exercises. Whether it is walking around the home for different chores or climbing the stairs to reach your office floor, these regular day activities still need energy to be done. NEAT helps to regulate our daily calorie expenditures and, in turn, keeps us active "metabolically".

Sleep Management:

The sleep-wake cycle is another significant factor in regulating your metabolic health. I can't stress enough the fact that we need to listen to and trust our body's natural cues. The natural biological clock is the key to keep not only your metabolism, but your whole body healthy and active. Sleep deprivation makes you feel hungrier without actually making you full- it disrupts your hunger hormones, leptin and ghrelin. This disruption, in turn, makes you feel hungrier without feeling satiety. Make sure to give your body rest and energy by sleeping for at least 7 hours daily.

Stress Management:

We all have read about stress and cortisol's effects on our metabolic health. So, to maintain a healthy metabolism, we need to keep our minds relaxed. We should engage in the practice of yoga and other meditating activities that could help to release pressure on our mind and hence maintain optimum levels of cortisol. By managing stress, we can ensure a healthy metabolism and give our body the gift of good energy.

Final points on maintaining optimum metabolism in the long run:

Metabolism accounts for all the chemical reactions going on inside our body. Research has shown a significant increase in metabolic diseases around the globe. Making lifestyle changes and following a good routine will help us prevent the risk of becoming a victim of such chronic diseases. We need to take care of our dietary habits, sleep schedules, and stress levels consistently and avoid quick fixes and fad diets. We should adopt long-term healthy habits and should focus on long-term results. Metabolic rates will increase and speed up by focusing on the above-mentioned lifestyle tips. Maintaining good metabolic health is the way to go for energy and weight regulation, as well as ensuring your body is providing maximum energy for daily activities and your lifestyle choices are enhancing your immune system.

CHAPTER 5:
ENERGIZING BREAKFASTS

1. Blueberry Banana Smoothie

Prep Time:	Cooking Time:	Servings:
8-10 min	0 min	1

Ingredients:

- ½ cup fresh or frozen blueberries
- ¼ cup baby spinach leaves
- ½ small banana, diced
- ½ cup unsweetened almond milk
- ¼ cup almond yogurt
- 1 tsp flax seeds

Instructions:

1. Combine all the ingredients.

2. Blend all the ingredients on high speed until you achieve a smooth and creamy consistency.

3. Transfer the smoothie into a glass and garnish with some blueberries on top.

4. Serve immediately.

Nutrition Facts (per serving):

Calories: 326, Carbohydrates: 64 g, Protein: 4 g, Fat: 7 g, Fiber: 12 g

2. Strawberry Almond Oats Smoothie

Prep Time:	Cooking Time:	Servings:
8-10 min	0 min	1

Ingredients:

- ½ cup strawberries
- 1 small banana, sliced
- ½ cup unsweetened almond milk
- 2 tbsp oats
- 1 tsp hemp seeds
- 5 g almonds, chopped

Instructions:

1. Combine all the ingredients.

2. Blend all the ingredients on high speed until you achieve a smooth and creamy consistency.

3. Transfer the smoothie into a glass and garnish with a sliced strawberry on top.

4. Serve immediately.

Nutrition Facts (per serving): Calories: 223, Carbohydrates: 38 g, Protein: 6 g, Fat: 8 g, Fiber: 12 g

3. Mixed Berries Smoothie Fusion

Prep Time:	Cooking Time:	Servings:
8-10 min	0 min	2

Ingredients:

- ½ cup raspberries
- ¼ cup strawberries
- ¼ cup blueberries
- ¼ cup baby spinach leaves
- 1 small banana, diced
- 1 cup unsweetened soy milk
- 5 g Brazil nuts
- 1 tsp chia seeds

Instructions:

1. Combine all the ingredients.

2. Blend all the ingredients on high speed until you achieve a smooth and creamy consistency.

3. Transfer the smoothie into a glass and garnish with some mixed berries on top.

4. Serve immediately.

Nutrition Facts (per serving): Calories: 170, Carbohydrates: 42 g, Protein: 12 g, Fat: 11 g, Fiber: 13 g

4. Green Avocado Smoothie

Prep Time:	Cooking Time:	Servings:
8-10 min	0 min	1-2

Ingredients:

- ½ cup avocado, chopped
- 1 small Granny Smith apple, chopped
- ¼ cup baby kale leaves, chopped
- ¼ cup pineapple chunks
- 1 cup coconut water
- 1 tsp raw honey
- 5 g walnuts

Instructions:

1. Combine all the ingredients.

2. Blend all the ingredients on high speed until you achieve a smooth and creamy consistency.

3. Transfer the smoothie into a glass and garnish with some pineapple chunks on top.

4. Serve immediately.

Nutrition Facts (per serving): Calories: 180, Carbohydrates: 48 g, Protein: 6 g, Fat: 12 g, Fiber: 14 g

5. Creamy Spinach and Pear Smoothie

Prep Time:	Cooking Time: 0 min	Servings:
8-10 min		1

Ingredients:

- ½ cup baby spinach leaves
- 1 medium pear, chopped
- ½ small banana, sliced
- ½ cup oat or soy milk
- ¼ cup Greek yogurt

- 1 tsp manuka honey
- 1 tsp flax seeds

Instructions:

1. Combine all the ingredients.

2. Blend all the ingredients on high speed until you achieve a smooth and creamy consistency.

3. Transfer the smoothie into a glass and garnish with some baby spinach leaves on top.

4. Serve immediately.

Nutrition Facts (per serving): Calories: 371, Carbohydrates: 75 g, Protein: 13 g, Fat: 4 g, Fiber: 12 g

6. Strawberry Smoothie Bowl with nuts and granola

Prep Time:	Cooking Time: 0 min	Servings:
8-10 min		1

Ingredients:

- 1 cup fresh or frozen strawberries
- ½ banana, diced
- ¼ cup almond milk
- 1/8 cup low-fat yogurt
- Pinch of cinnamon powder

For the topping:

- 2 tbsp granola
- 5 g walnuts
- 5 g almonds
- 1 tsp flax seeds
- 1-2 strawberry slices
- 1 tbsp acacia honey (for drizzling)

Instructions:

1. Combine all the ingredients.

2. Blend the strawberries, banana, almond milk, low-fat yogurt, and cinnamon powder on high speed until you achieve a smooth and creamy consistency.

3. Transfer the smoothie into a bowl and top it with granola, chopped nuts, strawberry slices, and flax seeds.

4. Drizzle 1 tbsp of acacia honey if desired.

Nutrition Facts (per serving): Calories: 318, Carbohydrates: 56 g, Protein: 7 g, Fat: 10 g, Fiber: 14 g

7. Quinoa High-Protein Breakfast Bowl

Prep Time:	Cooking Time: 0 min	Servings:
8-10 min		1

Ingredients:

- ½ cup cooked quinoa or ¼ cup dry quinoa of any preferred brand
- ½ cup Greek yogurt
- 1 tbsp nut butter of your choice
- ¼ cup blueberries
- 1 tsp chia seeds soaked in water for 5-10 minutes
- 1 tbsp acacia honey

Instructions:

1. Cook the quinoa as per package instructions.

2. Transfer the cooked quinoa into a serving bowl. Add the Greek yogurt, nut butter, blueberries, and chia seeds on top.

4. Drizzle 1 tbsp of acacia honey if desired.

Nutrition Facts (per serving): Calories: 430, Carbohydrates: 102 g, Protein: 28 g, Fat: 25 g, Fiber: 33 g

8. Overnight Chia seeds Breakfast Bowl

Prep Time:	Cooking Time: 0 min	Servings:
8-10 min		1

Ingredients:

- 2.5 tbsp chia seeds
- 200 ml almond or oat milk
- 50 ml Greek yogurt
- 2 tbsp rolled oats
- Pinch of cardamom powder
- Pinch of cinnamon powder
- 1 tbsp raw honey or stevia

For the topping:

- ¼ cup mixed berries
- ¼ cup pomegranate seeds
- 1 tbsp mixed nuts

Instructions:

1. Combine all the ingredients in a serving bowl. Mix them well to avoid clumping. Leave them overnight or for 4 hours.

2. Top the bowl with berries, pomegranate seeds, and mixed nuts and serve immediately.

Nutrition Facts (per serving): Calories: 272, Carbohydrates: 102 g, Protein: 14 g, Fat: 18 g, Fiber: 21 g

9. Oatmeal Breakfast Bowl

Prep Time:	Cooking Time: 12min	Servings:
5 min		1

Ingredients:

- ½ cup rolled oats
- 1 cup unsweetened almond or soy milk
- 1 tbsp chocolate-flavored protein powder

- ¼ cup spring water

For the topping:

- 1 tbsp dried cranberries
- ¼ cup fresh raspberries
- ¼ cup blueberries
- 5 g walnuts
- 1 tsp sunflower seeds
- 1 tsp manuka honey

Instructions:

1. Place the saucepan over medium heat. Add the water, and oats and cook it for 5 mins. Add the almond or soy milk and protein powder and cook until the oats are cooked properly.

2. Transfer the oatmeal into a serving bowl and top it with berries, walnuts, and sunflower seeds.

3. 3. Drizzle 1 tsp manuka honey over it and serve while warm.

Nutrition Facts (per serving): Calories: 430, Carbohydrates: 130 g, Protein: 37 g, Fat: 20 g, Fiber: 24 g

10. Scrambled Eggs and Veggie Breakfast Bowl

Prep Time:	Cooking Time: 10min	Servings:
10min		1

Ingredients:

- 2 medium eggs
- ½ cup fresh baby spinach leaves
- ½ cup cherry tomatoes
- ¼ cup red bell pepper
- ¼ cup broccoli florets
- ¼ cup feta cheese
- 1 tbsp black olives
- ¼ tsp sea salt
- ¼ tsp black pepper
- 1 tsp fresh parsley
- 1 tsp extra virgin olive oil

Instructions:

1. Heat the olive oil in a saucepan. Add the 2 beaten eggs with salt and pepper into them. Add fresh spinach leaves and cook them for 2-3 minutes on each side and make them scrambled.

2. Transfer the eggs into a serving bowl, and in the same pan, sauté the cherry tomatoes, bell pepper, and broccoli florets for 2-3 minutes.

3. Add the layer of sautéed veggies over the scrambled eggs. Top it with the black olives, feta cheese, and fresh parsley and serve.

Nutrition Facts (per serving): Calories: 320, Carbohydrates: 40 g, Protein: 34 g, Fat: 44 g, Fiber: 22 g

11. Hard Boiled Eggs Veggie Salad

Prep Time:	Cooking Time: 10min	Servings:
10min		1

Ingredients:

- 2 medium eggs
- ½ cup cherry tomatoes, chopped
- 1 medium cucumber, chopped
- ½ cup avocados, cubed
- ½ cup red onion, chopped

For the dressing:

- Juice of 1 lime
- ¼ tsp kosher salt
- ¼ tsp black pepper
- ¼ tsp sumac
- 1 tsp extra virgin olive oil
- Few cilantro leaves

Instructions:

1. Place the eggs in a saucepan half-filled with water. Boil the eggs for about 12 minutes. Place them in cold water and set them aside. Peel them and cut them in cubes.

2. Add the chopped cucumber, tomatoes, avocado and red onion to the cubed eggs.

3. Make a dressing by mixing the lime juice, kosher salt, black pepper, sumac, cilantro leaves and extra virgin olive oil.

4. Drizzle it over the egg and veggie mixture.

5. Serve immediately.

Nutrition Facts (per serving): Calories: 330, Carbohydrates: 25 g, Protein: 25 g, Fat: 22 g, Fiber: 12 g

12. Almond Yogurt Parfait With Assorted Fruits

Prep Time:	Cooking Time: 10min	Servings:
10min		1

Ingredients:

- 1 cup almond yogurt
- ½ cup raspberries
- ½ cup blueberries
- 2 kiwis, peeled and cubed
- 2 tbsp granola
- 2 tbsp mixed nuts
- 2 tsp chia seeds, soaked in water for 5-10 minutes
- 1 tbsp manuka honey (for drizzling)

Instructions:

1. Divide the almond yogurt into two serving bowls.

2. In one bowl add the ¼ cup almond yogurt, ½ tbsp granola, 1/8 cup raspberries and blueberries, ½ kiwi, ¼ tsp chia seed. Repeat the same layer to complete one yogurt parfait bowl.

3. Repeat the same process on the other bowl.

4. Drizzle manuka honey on top of the parfait bowls.

5. Refrigerate for 1 hour. Serve chill.

Nutrition Facts (per serving): Calories: 390, Carbohydrates: 65 g, Protein: 17 g, Fat: 22 g, Fiber: 15 g

13. Overnight Oatmeal High-Fiber Breakfast

Prep Time:	Cooking Time: 10min	Servings:
10min		1

Ingredients:

- 1 cup rolled oats
- 1 cup unsweetened soy milk
- ¼ cup spring water
- 1 tbsp chia seeds
- 2 tsp vanilla extract
- ½ cup blueberries
- ¼ cup Graham crackers (store-bought)
- 5 g pecans, crushed

- 5 g almonds, chopped
- 5 g walnuts, chopped
- 1 tsp flax seeds

Instructions:

1. In a medium bowl, add the oats, soy milk, spring water, and chia seeds. Mix it well. Cover it with an air-tight lid and put it in the refrigerator for about 4 hours or overnight.

2. In the morning, take this bowl out and add the fresh blueberries, mixed and chopped nuts, and flax seeds.

3. Serve immediately.

Nutrition Facts (per serving): Calories: 440, Carbohydrates: 70 g, Protein: 23 g, Fat: 23 g, Fiber: 16

14. Cinnamon Sweet Potato Oatmeal Pancakes

Prep Time:	Cooking Time: 10min	Servings:
10min		1

Ingredients:

- 1 cup rolled oats
- 1 cup sweet potato puree of any preferred brand
- ½ cup unsweetened milk
- ½ tsp cinnamon powder
- 2 medium eggs
- 2 tbsp manuka honey
- 2 tsp baking powder
- 2 tbsp sesame seeds

For the topping:

- 2 tbsp almond butter
- ½ medium Fuji apple, diced

Instructions:

1. Combine the wet ingredients, eggs, almond milk, and honey. Mix it well and leave it for 5 minutes.

2. Add the oats, baking powder, and cinnamon powder to it. Then, gradually add the sweet potato puree.

3. Heat olive oil in a non-stick pan. Add approximately 1/3 of the batter into it with the help of a spoon and cook it for 3-4 minutes on one side.

4. Repeat the same process until the batter is finished.

5. Spread a layer of almond butter on each pancake. Top it with the diced apples and drizzle raw honey over it.

Nutrition Facts (per serving): Calories: 550, Carbohydrates: 78 g, Protein: 23 g, Fat: 30 g, Fiber: 13 g

15. Muesli and Oatmeal Waffle With Apricots

Prep Time:	Cooking Time: 10min	Servings:
10min		1

Ingredients:

- 1 cup oat flour
- ½ cup muesli of any preferred brand with no added sugar
- 1 medium egg
- ½ cup almond or soy milk
- 1 tsp baking powder
- ½ tsp cinnamon powder
- ¼ tsp nutmeg powder

For the topping:

- 5 g hazelnuts
- 5 g walnuts
- 5 g Medjool dates
- ½ cup apricots

Instructions:

1. Preheat the waffle machine for about 10 minutes.

2. Combine all the ingredients mentioned and make a batter.

3. Transfer the batter to a waffle machine and spread it. Close the waffle machine gradually and cook until it gets a light golden color.

4. Repeat the same process until the batter is finished.

5. Top it with the mentioned chopped nuts and apricots.

6. Serve immediately.

Nutrition Facts (per serving): Calories: 400, Carbohydrates: 55 g, Protein: 17 g, Fat: 20 g, Fiber:

CHAPTER 6:
POWER LUNCHES

1. Sesame Chicken with Sauteed Veggies

Prep Time:	Cooking Time:	Servings:
10min	20min	2

Ingredients:

- 1 large chicken breast
- 1 tbsp extra virgin olive oil
- 1 cup broccoli florets, chopped
- ½ cup Brussels sprouts, chopped
- Salt and pepper as per taste
- ½ tsp red chili flakes
- 1 tsp sesame seeds
- 1 cup rice, brown or white, of any preferred brand

For the honey sesame oil-infused sauce:

- 2 tbsp honey
- ¼ cup chicken broth
- 1 tbsp sesame oil
- ¼ tsp paprika powder
- ¼ tsp black pepper
- 1 tbsp Worcestershire sauce
- 1 tsp corn flour

Instructions:

1. Mix all the honey sesame oil-infused sauce ingredients and set it aside.

2. Heat the olive oil in a non-stick pan over medium heat. Season the chicken with the salt, pepper, and red chili flakes. Cook the chicken breast for 7-8 minutes on each side or until it is cooked properly.

3. Boil the rice as per package instructions.

4. In the same pan, sauté broccoli and Brussels sprouts for about 2 minutes.

5. Divide the boiled rice into two serving.

6. Garnish with sesame seeds and spring onions.

Nutrition Facts (per serving): Calories: 410, Carbohydrates: 65 g, Protein: 45 g, Fat: 31 g, Fiber: 12 g

2. Garlic Salmon Patties With Coleslaw Salad

Prep Time:	Cooking Time:	Servings:
15min	15min	1

Ingredients:

- 1 can salmon, fresh or canned
- ¼ cup almond flour
- 1 small egg
- Juice of 1 lime
- ½ tbsp fresh parsley
- ½ tbsp fresh chives, chopped

- 1/8 cup onion, minced
- ¼ tsp Kosher salt
- ¼ tsp freshly ground black pepper
- 1 tbsp extra virgin olive oil

For the coleslaw salad:

- ½ cup purple and green cabbage
- 1 green onion, chopped and roots

For the dressing:

- 2 tbsp low-fat mayonnaise
- 3 tbsp Greek yogurt
- 1/8 tsp garlic powder
- ¼ tsp black pepper

Instructions:

1. In a medium bowl, combine all the ingredients of the salmon patties. Mix until all the ingredients are well combined.

2. Shape the mixture and form 2-3 medium-sized patties.

3. Heat the olive oil in a non-stick pan until they get a nice golden brown color.

4. Assemble the veggies for the coleslaw salad and add the dressing over it.

5. Place the salmon patties over it.

6. Garnish with green onions and serve.

Nutrition Facts (per serving):

Calories: 410, Carbohydrates: 65 g, Protein: 45 g, Fat: 31 g, Fiber: 12 g

3. Whole Wheat Tuna Wrap

Prep Time:	Cooking Time: 0min	Servings:
15min		1

Ingredients:

- 1 whole wheat tortilla wrap
- 1 can cooked tuna
- ¼ cup cucumber, chopped
- 1 small tomato, chopped
- Fresh lettuce leaves
- Salt and freshly ground black pepper as per taste
- 1 tsp lime juice

For the sauce:

- 2 tbsp light mayonnaise
- 2 tbsp Greek yogurt
- 1 tsp extra virgin olive oil
- Pinch of garlic powder

Instructions:

1. Place the whole wheat tortilla wraps on a serving plate.

2. Spread the sauce on them, followed by the cooked tuna, chopped cucumber, tomato, and lettuce leaves.

3. Cut in half if desired.

4. Serve immediately.

Nutrition Facts (per serving):

Calories: 411, Carbohydrates: 36 g, Protein: 40 g, Fat: 14 g, Fiber: 6 g

4. Grilled Turkey And Veggie Wrap

Prep Time:	Cooking Time: 0min	Servings:
15min		2

Ingredients:

- 3 slices of turkey breast, cooked and grilled
- ½ medium zucchini, chopped
- ¼ cup red or yellow bell pepper
- ¼ cup boiled chickpeas, canned
- Fresh lettuce leaves
- ¼ cup cherry tomato, chopped
- 1 whole wheat tortilla wrap

For the sauce:

- 2 tbsp light mayonnaise
- 2 tbsp Greek yogurt
- 1 tsp extra virgin olive oil
- 1 tbsp Dijon mustard sauce
- 1 tsp hot sauce
- 1 tsp balsamic vinegar

Instructions:

1. Place the whole wheat tortilla wrap on a serving plate.

2. In a non-stick pan, sauté the veggies for 2-3 mins.

3. Spread the sauce on the wrap followed by the cooked turkey, then add a layer of the sauteed veggies.

4. Cut in half if desired.

5. Serve immediately.

Nutrition Facts (per serving):

Calories: 215, Carbohydrates: 24 g, Protein: 16 g, Fat: 8 g, Fiber: 4 g

5. Quinoa Black Bean Salad With Lime Dressing

Prep Time:	Cooking Time: 0min	Servings:
15min		2

Ingredients:

- ½ cup cooked quinoa
- ½ cup black beans, canned and rinsed
- ½ cup chickpeas, canned
- ½ cup fresh mango chunks
- ½ cup avocado, chopped

For the dressing:

- 1 tbsp lime juice
- Pinch of sea salt
- ¼ tsp black pepper
- Few cilantro leaves

Instructions:

1. Mix the dressing ingredients in a small bowl and set it aside.

2. Add the cooked quinoa, black beans, chickpeas, mango chunks and avocado in a bowl.

3. Add the lime seasoning over it.

4. Serve immediately.

Nutrition Facts (per serving):

Calories: 203, Carbohydrates: 36 g, Protein: 9 g, Fat: 7 g, Fiber: 9 g

6. Green Spinach Pasta With Creamy Parmesan Sauce

Prep Time:	Cooking Time: 0min	Servings:
15min		2

Ingredients:

- 1 cup whole wheat pasta of your preferred shape
- ½ cup baby spinach leaves

For the sauce:

- 2 tbsp unsalted butter
- 1-2 cloves of garlic
- 2 tbsp all-purpose flour
- ½ cup chicken broth
- ½ cup almond milk
- ¼ cup parmesan cheese
- ¼ tsp dried oregano
- ¼ tsp parsley
- ¼ tsp black pepper
- Salt as per taste

Instructions:

1. Boil the pasta as per package instructions.

2. Heat the butter in a non-stick pan and roast the all-purpose flour until it turns golden brown.

3. Add the chicken broth and almond milk and whisk continuously for a few minutes until the sauce starts to thicken.

4. Add the herbs mentioned in the ingredients and the parmesan cheese. Then add the spinach leaves and cook for 2 minutes.

5. Add the drained pasta to it and serve warm.

Nutrition Facts (per serving): Calories: 293, Carbohydrates: 27 g, Protein: 11 g, Fat: 16 g, Fiber: 3 g

7. Peach And Avocado Salad With Feta Cheese Topping

Prep Time:	Cooking Time: 0min	Servings:
15min		2

Ingredients:

- 1 cup baby spinach leaves
- 2 large peaches, sliced or chopped

- ½ avocado, sliced
- ¼ cup crumbled feta cheese
- 5 g walnuts, chopped
- 5 g pecans, chopped

For the dressing:

- 1 tbsp acacia honey
- 1/8 tsp black pepper
- 1 tbsp apple cider vinegar
- 1/8 teaspoon sea salt

Instructions:

1. Mix the dressing ingredients in a small bowl and set it aside.

2. Combine all the salad ingredients in a bowl.

3. Add the crumbled feta cheese and prepared dressing with chopped nuts over it.

4. Mix everything and serve.

Nutrition Facts (per serving):

Calories: 200, Carbohydrates: 30 g, Protein: 5 g, Fat: 13 g, Fiber: 5 g

8. Blueberry And Arugula Salad With Cheese

Prep Time:	Cooking Time: 0min	Servings:
15min		2

Ingredients:

- 1 cup fresh blueberries
- ½ cup strawberries, sliced
- 1 small apple of any variety, sliced
- ½ cup arugula
- ½ cup parmesan or feta cheese
- 1 tsp flax seeds

For the dressing:

- ¼ cup Greek yogurt
- 1 tsp raw honey

Instructions:

1. Combine all the ingredients in a serving bowl.

2. Toss them well and serve the delicious salad.

Nutrition Facts (per serving): Calories: 187, Carbohydrates: 30 g, Protein: 14 g, Fat: 8 g, Fiber: 3 g

9. Crunchy Strawberry Spinach Salad

Prep Time:	Cooking Time: 0min	Servings:
15min		2

Ingredients:

- 1 cup strawberries, halved

- ½ cup baby spinach leaves
- ¼ cup goat cheese
- 5 g almonds, chopped
- 5 g Brazil nuts, chopped
- 5 g walnuts, chopped

Instructions:

1. Combine all the ingredients in a serving bowl.

2. Garnish with the chopped nuts and serve.

Nutrition Facts (per serving): Calories: 124, Carbohydrates: 9 g, Protein: 5 g, Fat: 8 g, Fiber: 2 g

10. Mixed Beans And Veggie Salad

Prep Time: 15min	Cooking Time: 0min	Servings: 2

Ingredients:

- ½ cup white kidney beans, canned
- ½ cup red kidney beans, canned
- ½ cup chickpeas, canned and rinsed
- ½ cup onion, chopped
- 1 cup cucumber, chopped
- ½ cup tomatoes, chopped
- ½ cup lettuce leaves, chopped

For the dressing:

- 1 tbsp lime juice
- Pinch of sea salt
- ¼ tsp black pepper
- Few cilantro leaves

Instructions:

1. Mix the dressing ingredients in a small bowl and set it aside.

2. Add the beans and veggies in a bowl.

3. Add the dressing over it.

4. Toss well and serve.

Nutrition Facts (per serving): Calories: 192, Carbohydrates: 37 g, Protein: 12 g, Fat: 2 g, Fiber: 10 g

11. Edamame Beans Cucumber Kale Salad

Prep Time: 15min	Cooking Time: 0min	Servings: 2

Ingredients:

- ½ cup edamame beans
- ¼ cup green baby kale leaves
- ¼ cup purple kale leaves
- 1 medium cucumber, chopped

- ½ ripe avocado, chopped
- 1 tsp apple cider vinegar
- ¼ tsp black pepper
- ¼ tsp sea salt

Instructions:

1. Combine all the ingredients in a bowl.

2. Drizzle the apple cider vinegar over it.

3. Mix to combine, and serve.

Nutrition Facts (per serving): Calories: 252, Carbohydrates: 25.1 g, Protein: 14 g, Fat: 15.2 g, Fiber: 12.1 g

12. Grilled Chicken Breast With Avocado And Pomegranate Seeds

Prep Time: 10min	Cooking Time: 17 min	Servings: 2

Ingredients:

- 1 chicken breast
- ½ ripe avocado, sliced
- ½ cup pomegranate seeds
- ½ cup tomatoes, sliced
- 1 cup baby spinach leaves

For the grilled chicken seasoning:

- Salt and black pepper as per taste
- Juice of 1 lime
- 1 tsp soya sauce
- 1 tbsp extra virgin olive oil

Instructions:

1. Cook the chicken breast over medium heat in a non-stick pan for 7-8 minutes on each side or until cooked properly. Cut into slices or chunks.

2. Add the remaining ingredients in a bowl.

3. Mix them well.

4. Serve & enjoy.

Nutrition Facts (per serving): Calories: 633, Carbohydrates: 31 g, Protein: 58.7 g, Fat: 32 g, Fiber: 10.1 g

13. Broccoli Veggie Pasta Salad With Pine Nuts

Prep Time: 15min	Cooking Time: 20 min	Servings: 2

Ingredients:

- 1 cup fusilli pasta, boiled
- ½ cup peas, canned
- ¼ cup arugula
- ½ cup broccoli
- 2 tbsp green olives

- 5 g pine nuts

For the dressing:

- 1 tbsp lime juice
- Pinch of sea salt
- ¼ tsp black pepper
- Few cilantro leaves

Instructions:

1. Boil the pasta as per package instructions. Mix the dressing ingredients in a small bowl and set it aside.

2. Saute the broccoli in a pan for 1-2 minutes.

3. Add the pasta and veggies in a bowl.

4. Add the dressing and pine nuts over it.

5. Serve immediately.

Nutrition Facts (per serving): Calories: 531.5, Carbohydrates: 64 g, Protein: 14 g, Fat: 23 g, Fiber: 10.15

CHAPTER 7:
DINNERS FOR SPEEDING UP YOUR METABOLISM

1. Greek Turkey Lettuce Rolls

Prep Time:	Cooking Time: 5min	Servings:
10min		2

Ingredients:

- 100 g ground turkey breast
- ½ cucumber, diced
- 1 tbsp olive oil
- Romaine lettuce leaves
- 1/4 cup crumbled feta cheese
- 1 teaspoon dried oregano
- Salt and pepper to taste

Instructions:

1. Heat the olive oil in a pan, and add the turkey meat to it. Then add the feta cheese, oregano, salt and pepper.

2. Stir well so all seasonings are combined with the meat.

3. Wash and dry the lettuce leaves.

4. Add the meat to the Romaine lettuce leaves, and add a layer of diced cucumber onto them.

5. Fold and roll the leaves. Serve and enjoy!

Nutrition Facts (per serving): Calories: 191, Carbohydrates: 4 g, Protein: 18 g, Fat: 12 g, Fiber: 1 g

2. Seared Scallops With Spinach

Prep Time:	Cooking Time: 5min	Servings:
10min		2

Ingredients:

- 6 scallops
- 1 tbsp olive oil
- 1 cup spinach
- 1 clove garlic, minced
- 1 tbsp lemon juice
- Salt and pepper to taste

Instructions:

1. Wash the scallops properly, and dry them. Next, season them with salt and pepper.

2. Add the olive oil to a pan, and sear the scallops.

3. Stir in the minced garlic and lemon juice. Keep cooking for 3-4 minutes.

4. Take the scallops out onto a plate, and in the same pan, add the spinach, and sauté it.

5. Place the scallops over the sautéed spinach, and sprinkle with parmesan cheese. Serve and enjoy!

Nutrition Facts (per serving): Calories: 221, Carbohydrates: 6 g, Protein: 35 g, Fat: 10 g, Fiber: 12 g

3. Chicken Zucchini Frittata Casserole

Prep Time: 20min	Cooking Time: 35min	Servings: 2

Ingredients:

- 1 chicken breast
- 1 zucchini, sliced
- 1 small onion, chopped
- 1 tbsp ginger-garlic paste
- ¼ cup mozzarella cheese
- 2 tbsp cheddar cheese
- 2 tbsp parmesan cheese
- ¼ cup tomato sauce
- ¼ cup marinara sauce

Instructions:

1. Preheat the oven to 375 degrees F.

2. Take a large pan and grease it with olive oil. Saute the onion, and add the ginger-garlic paste. Then, add the chicken and zucchini and cook until both the meat and veggies become tender.

3. In a large baking bowl, layer the chicken, zucchini, and all kinds of cheese. Then, add the tomato and marinara sauce on top.

4. Bake for 30 minutes, and the dish is ready. Serve and enjoy!

Nutrition Facts (per serving): Calories: 270, Carbohydrates: 12 g, Protein: 43 g, Fat: 14 g, Fiber: 2 g

4. Grilled Mahi-Mahi With Mango Salsa

Prep Time: 20min	Cooking Time: 12min	Servings: 2

Ingredients:

- 1 mahi-mahi fillet
- 1 tsp olive oil
- 1 tsp lime juice
- 1 tsp garlic, minced
- 1 tsp oregano
- Salt and pepper
- ½ mango, diced
- ¼ cup red onions
- 1 tbsp lemon juice

Instructions:

1. Start the grill, and pre-heat it to medium heat.

2. Take a small bowl, and add the fillet with the olive oil, garlic, lime juice, and oregano. Add salt and pepper to taste. Mix it well to marinate for 15-20 minutes.

3. Grill the fillet for 5-6 minutes per side or until perfectly cooked.

4. Meanwhile, take another bowl, and add the mango, red onions, and lemon juice. Combine well.

5. Take the grilled fillet out of your serving plate, and top it with mango salsa. Serve and enjoy!

Nutrition Facts (per serving): Calories: 240, Carbohydrates: 10 g, Protein: 35 g, Fat: 12 g, Fiber: 2 g

5. Slow-Cooked Lemon Basil Chicken

Prep Time: 15min	Cooking Time: 4 hrs	Servings: 2

Ingredients:

- 1 chicken breast
- 1 tbsp olive oil
- Fresh basil
- 1 tbsp lemon juice
- 1 tsp dried thyme
- Salt and pepper

Instructions:

1. Marinate the chicken breast with salt and pepper. Also, add thyme. Mix it well and leave it for 10 minutes.

2. Turn on the flame. In a slow cooker, add the olive oil, basil, and lemon juice. Mix well.

3. Then, add the chicken and let it cook for 4 hours.

4. Take it out in your serving bowl. Serve hot, and enjoy!

Nutrition Facts (per serving): Calories: 170, Carbohydrates: 0 g, Protein: 37 g, Fat: 8 g, Fiber: 1 g

6. Slow-Cooked Chicken Fajitas

Prep Time: 15min	Cooking Time: 4 hrs	Servings: 2

Ingredients:

- 1 chicken breast
- ½ onion, sliced
- ½ bell pepper, sliced
- 1 clove garlic, minced
- 1 tsp cumin powder
- 1 tsp red chilli powder
- ½ tsp paprika
- Salt and pepper
- 2 small tortilla wraps

Instructions:

1. Season the chicken with all the spices and salt and pepper.

2. In a slow cooker, add the marinated chicken along with the veggies and minced garlic. Cook it on low heat for almost 4 hours.

3. Then, shred the cooked chicken using your hands into thin threads.

4. Warm the tortilla wraps, and add the shredded chicken to them. Next, add the vegetable mixture, and any desired toppings.

Nutrition Facts (per serving): Calories: 320, Carbohydrates: 30 g, Protein: 37 g, Fat: 8 g, Fiber: 4 g

1. Take a pan, and add olive oil into it. Put it over medium flame.

2. Then, add the eggplant and cooked chickpeas together, and sauté them. Add seasonings, and mix well to combine.

3. Then, add the diced tomato and chicken broth, and keep the pan to simmer for almost 15 minutes.

4. Serve the stew hot, and enjoy!

Nutrition Facts (per serving): Calories: 140, Carbohydrates: 25 g, Protein: 10 g, Fat: 3 g, Fiber: 6 g

7. Eggplant And Chickpea Stew

Prep Time:	Cooking Time:	Servings:
20min	30min	2

Ingredients:

- ½ eggplant, diced
- ½ cup cooked chickpeas
- 1 tomato, diced
- ¼ cup chicken broth
- 1 tsp paprika
- Salt and pepper

Instructions:

8. Grilled Tofu And Quinoa Bowl

Prep Time:	Cooking Time:	Servings:
15min	20min	2

Ingredients:

- ½ tofu
- ½ cup cooked quinoa
- 1 tbsp olive oil
- 1 tbsp soy sauce
- ½ cup mixed veggies (broccoli, carrot, bell peppers)
- 1 tsp sesame seeds
- Salt and pepper

Instructions:

1. Start by grilling the tofu after greasing it with olive oil. Cook for 3-5 minutes on both sides until tender and golden brown.

2 Take a pan and place it over medium-low flame. Add the olive oil, and then add the mixed veggies to sauté them for 2-3 minutes for a crispy feel.

3. Add the quinoa to the sautéed veggies, then stir in the soy sauce, and mix well to combine.

4. Finally, add the grilled tofu, and season the dish with salt and pepper according to taste.

5. Take them all out on the serving plate and sprinkle sesame seeds on top, serve and enjoy!

Nutrition Facts (per serving): Calories: 320, Carbohydrates: 25 g, Protein: 20 g, Fat: 17 g, Fiber: 6 g

9. Moroccan Lamb With Cauliflower Rice

Prep Time:	Cooking Time: 4-5 hrs	Servings:
10min		2

Ingredients:

- 1 lamb chop
- ½ tsp cumin powder
- ½ tsp coriander powder
- ½ tsp cinnamon powder
- 1 garlic clove
- 1 tsp grated ginger
- ¼ tsp cayenne pepper
- 1 tsp olive oil
- ½ cup cooked cauliflower rice

Instructions:

1. Take a large pan and add oil to it. Add the lamb chop into the pan and let it brown on both sides. Turn off the flame.

2. Now, add this browned lamb chop into a slow cooker, and add the ginger, garlic, and all mentioned spices. Mix well.

3. Cook on low heat for 4-5 hours. Serve the slow-cooked lamb chop over the sautéed cauliflower rice. Enjoy!

Nutrition Facts (per serving): Calories: 240, Carbohydrates: 5 g, Protein: 35 g, Fat: 14 g, Fiber: 2 g

10. Slow-cooked barbecue Chicken

Prep Time:	Cooking Time: 5 hrs	Servings:
10min		2

Ingredients:

- 1 chicken breast
- Low-sugar barbecue sauce

Instructions:

1. Marinate the chicken breast with rich barbecue sauce.

2. Transfer the marinated chicken to a slow cooker. Cook for 5 hours.

3. Cut the chicken into bite-size chops. Serve with a side of coleslaw.

Nutrition Facts (per serving): Calories: 140, Carbohydrates: 5 g, Protein: 30 g, Fat: 3 g, Fiber: 0 g

11. Avocado Tuna Salad

Prep Time:	Cooking Time:	Servings:
15min	0min	2

Ingredients:

- 1 can of tuna (in water)
- ½ avocado, mashed
- ½ small onion, diced
- ½ cup of mixed greens
- 2 tsp lime juice
- Salt and pepper

Instructions:

1. Combine the tuna, avocado, onion, and mixed greens in a salad bowl.

2. Add the lime juice to the bowl. Toss well to combine. Add salt and pepper according to taste.

3. Serve and enjoy!

Nutrition Facts (per serving): Calories: 270, Carbohydrates: 10 g, Protein: 35 g, Fat: 15 g, Fiber: 7 g

12. Turkey Meatballs With Zucchini Noodles

Prep Time:	Cooking Time:	Servings:
15min	15min	2

Ingredients:

- 100 g ground turkey
- 1 egg
- 1 zucchini, spiralized
- 1 clove garlic, minced
- ¼ cup breadcrumbs
- 1/3 cup low-sugar marinara sauce
- 2 tbsp parsley, chopped
- 3 tbsp grated parmesan cheese
- Salt and pepper

Instructions:

1. Preheat the oven to 400 degrees F.

2. Season the turkey meat with garlic, bread crumbs, egg, parsley, cheese, marinara sauce, salt and pepper. Mix well till all the ingredients are properly combined with the meat.

3. Now, make small-ball-sized (about 1 ½ inch in diameter) meatballs of the marinated turkey meat.

4. Line a baking tray with parchment paper. Place the meatballs over it and bake for 15-20 mins or until they are properly cooked.

5. Now, take a pan, and sauté the zucchini noodles in it for 4 minutes, until they are halfway tender.

6. Add the baked meatballs to the skillet and add the marinara sauce to it. Mix well.

7. Season with salt and pepper, take out in the serving dish, and enjoy!

Nutrition Facts (per serving): Calories: 320, Carbohydrates: 20 g, Protein: 37 g, Fat: 18 g, Fiber: 4 g

13. Herbed Chicken Thighs With Cauliflower Mash

Prep Time:	Cooking Time:	Servings:
15min	30min	2

Ingredients:

- 2 skinless chicken thighs
- 1 tbsp unsalted butter
- 1 tbsp rosemary
- 1 tbsp fresh thyme
- 1 garlic clove
- Salt and pepper
- ½ head of cauliflower
- ¼ cup Greek yogurt

Instructions:

1. Preheat the oven to 400 degrees F. Marinate the chicken thighs with the butter, rosemary, thyme, and garlic. Also, add salt and pepper to taste. Mix well.

2. Place the marinated chicken thighs on a baking sheet lined with parchment paper.

3. Bake in a preheated oven for 25 minutes, until they're properly baked.

4. Mash the cauliflower in a blender so that it resembles rice. Then, steam the cauliflower with Greek yoghurt for a creamy touch.

5. Serve the baked thighs over this cauliflower mash. Enjoy!

Nutrition Facts (per serving): Calories: 340, Carbohydrates: 10 g, Protein: 40 g, Fat: 20 g, Fiber:

CHAPTER 8:
SNACKS FOR ENERGY

1. Homemade Flaxseed And Oats Energy-Rich Bars

Prep Time:	Cooking Time: 0min	Servings:
15min		2

Ingredients:

- 7-8 Medjool dates
- ½ cup almonds
- ¼ cup rolled oats
- ½ cup peanut butter
- ½ tsp ground cinnamon
- 1 tbsp honey
- 1 tsp flax seeds

Instructions:

1. Combine all the ingredients in a food processor.

2. Turn on the food processor and process this mixture for 30 seconds.

3. Place this mixture on a baking sheet lined with parchment paper and press it firmly with the help of a spoon.

4. Put this baking sheet in the refrigerator for 2 hours.

5. Take it out of the fridge and cut the mixture into equal bars.

Nutrition Facts (per serving): Calories: 420, Carbohydrates: 40 g, Protein: 12 g, Fat: 24 g, Fiber: 8 g

2. Homemade Mixed Nuts And Muesli Energy Bites

Prep Time:	Cooking Time: 0min	Servings:
15min		2

Ingredients:

- ¼ cup sunflower seeds
- ¼ cup pumpkin seeds
- ¼ cup almonds
- ¼ cup muesli
- 1 tbsp flaxseeds
- 1 tbsp sesame seeds
- 15 g unsalted butter
- 40 ml raw or acacia honey
- ½ tsp vanilla extract
- 2 tbsp shredded coconut

Instructions:

1. Combine all the ingredients in a food processor.

2. Turn on the food processor and process this mixture for 30 seconds.

3. Place this mixture on a baking sheet lined with parchment paper and press it firmly with the help of a spoon.

4. Put this baking sheet in the refrigerator for 2 hours.

5. Take it out of the fridge and cut the mixture into equal bites.

6. Serve and enjoy the energy bites.

Nutrition Facts (per serving): Calories: 250, Carbohydrates: 40 g, Protein: 15 g, Fat: 35 g, Fiber: 10 g

3. Homemade Dates And Dried Cherries Energy Bars

Prep Time: 15min	Cooking Time: 0min	Servings: 2

Ingredients:

- 5-6 Medjool dates
- ¼ cup dried cherries
- ¼ cup dried raisins
- ¼ cup dried figs
- ¼ cup walnuts
- 2 tbsp granola

Instructions:

1. Combine all the ingredients in a food processor.

2. Turn on the food processor and process this mixture for 30 seconds.

3. Place this mixture on a baking sheet lined with parchment paper and press it firmly with the help of a spoon.

4. Put this baking sheet in the refrigerator for 2 hours.

5. Take it out of the fridge and cut the mixture into equal bars.

6. Serve and enjoy the energy bars.

Nutrition Facts (per serving): Calories: 320, Carbohydrates: 45 g, Protein: 5 g, Fat: 16 g, Fiber: 8 g

4. Homemade Dates And Dried Fruits Energy Bars

Prep Time: 15min	Cooking Time: 0min	Servings: 2

Ingredients:

- 5-6 Medjool dates
- ¼ cup dried apples
- ¼ cup dried apricots
- 5 g walnuts
- 5 g cashews
- 2 tbsp shredded coconut
- ½ tsp cinnamon powder
- ¼ cup grated carrot

- 1 tsp sesame seeds
- 1 tsp raw honey

Instructions:

1. Combine all the ingredients in a food processor.

2. Turn on the food processor and process this mixture for 30 seconds.

3. Place this mixture on a baking sheet lined with parchment paper and press it firmly with the help of a spoon.

4. Put this baking sheet in the refrigerator for 2 hours.

5. Take it out of the fridge and cut the mixture into equal bars.

6. Serve and enjoy the energy bars.

Nutrition Facts (per serving): Calories: 370, Carbohydrates: 45 g, Protein: 5 g, Fat: 20 g, Fiber: 10 g

5. Homemade Almond And Oats Energy Bars

Prep Time:	Cooking Time: 0min	Servings:
15min		2

Ingredients:

- ½ cup almonds
- ¼ cup oats
- ¼ cup granola
- 2 tbsp raw honey
- 1 tbsp almond butter
- 1 tsp almond extract
- 1 tbsp coconut oil
- 1/2 cup dried cranberries
- 2 tbsp pumpkin seeds

Instructions:

1. Combine all the ingredients in a food processor.

2. Turn on the food processor and process this mixture for 30 seconds.

3. Place this mixture on a baking sheet lined with parchment paper and press it firmly with the help of a spoon. Cut the mixture into equal bars.

4. Roll the energy bars in pumpkin seeds and coat them properly.

5. Put this baking sheet in the refrigerator for 2 hours.

6. Serve and enjoy the energy bars.

Nutrition Facts (per serving): Calories: 320, Carbohydrates: 30 g, Protein: 8 g, Fat: 20 g, Fiber: 8 g

6. Oats And Hemp Seeds Energy Bites

Prep Time:	Cooking Time: 0min	Servings:
15min		2

Ingredients:

- ¼ cup rolled oats
- 1/8 cup dark chocolate chips
- ¼ cup peanut butter
- 1/8 cup raw honey
- 1/8 cup ground flaxseeds
- 1 tsp vanilla extract
- Pinch of cardamom powder
- Pinch of nutmeg powder
- 2 tbsp hemp seeds

Instructions:

1. Combine all the ingredients in a medium bowl.

2. Roll the mixture into a ball or bite shape with the help of your hands greased with olive oil. Coat the balls with the hemp seeds.

3. Place the balls on a parchment paper-lined baking sheet.

4. Refrigerate them for 2 hours so that they are set properly.

6. Serve and enjoy the energy bars.

Nutrition Facts (per serving): Calories: 320, Carbohydrates: 12 g, Protein: 12 g, Fat: 22 g, Fiber: 6 g

7. Oats And Peach Fusion Smoothie

Prep Time:	Cooking Time: 0min	Servings:
15min		2

Ingredients:

- ½ cup almond milk
- ½ cup fresh or frozen peaches
- 2 tbsp oats
- ¼ cup Greek yogurt
- 5 g walnuts
- 1 tsp flaxseeds
- 1 tsp raw honey

Instructions:

1. Combine all the ingredients in a blender.

2. Blend all ingredients quickly until you achieve a smooth and creamy consistency.

3. Transfer the smoothie into a glass and garnish with peach chunks.

Nutrition Facts (per serving): Calories: 220, Carbohydrates: 35 g, Protein: 15 g, Fat: 10 g, Fiber: 6 g

8. Fiber-Rich Almond Chocolate Smoothie Bowl

Prep Time:	Cooking Time: 0min	Servings:
15min		2

Ingredients:

- 1 small banana, diced
- ½ cup unsweetened almond milk
- ¼ cup almond yogurt
- 1 tsp raw honey

For the topping:

- ¼ cup strawberries, halved
- ¼ cup raspberries
- ½ small banana, diced
- 1 tbsp granola
- 1 tbsp mixed nuts

Instructions:

1. Blend all the ingredients quickly until you achieve a smooth and creamy consistency.

2. Transfer the smoothie into a bowl.

3. Add the topping over it.

Nutrition Facts (per serving): Calories: 170, Carbohydrates: 30 g, Protein: 3 g, Fat: 8 g, Fiber: 6 g

9. Lime And Paprika-Seasoned Chickpeas

Prep Time:	Cooking Time: 0min	Servings:
7-10min		2

Ingredients:

- 1 cup chickpeas, canned
- 1 tbsp lime juice
- ¼ tsp paprika powder
- Few fresh cilantro leaves

Instructions:

1. Add the chickpeas to a medium bowl.

2. Season them with lime juice, paprika powder, and cilantro leaves.

3. Serve immediately.

Nutrition Facts (per serving): Calories: 110, Carbohydrates: 20 g, Protein: 5 g, Fat: 2 g, Fiber: 5 g

10. Almond Raspberry Smoothie

Prep Time:	Cooking Time: 0min	Servings:
7-10min		1

Ingredients:

- ½ cup fresh or frozen raspberries
- 1/2 small banana, diced
- ½ cup almond milk
- 1 tsp hemp seeds
- 5 g walnuts
- 1 tbsp muesli
- Ice cubes as needed

Instructions:

1. Combine all the ingredients in a blender.

2. Blend at high speed until you achieve a smooth and creamy consistency.

3. Serve and garnish with some raspberries.

Nutrition Facts (per serving): Calories: 170, Carbohydrates: 25 g, Protein: 3 g, Fat: 8 g, Fiber: 8 g

11. Banana Oatmeal Cookies

Prep Time:	Cooking Time: 15 min	Servings:
7-10min		2

Ingredients:

- 1 large ripe banana, mashed
- ¼ cup oats
- 1 tbsp almond butter
- 1 tbsp raw honey
- ¼ tsp cocoa powder
- 1 tbsp dried raisins
- 1 tsp dark chocolate chips

Instructions:

1. Mash the banana in a small bowl with the help of a fork.

2. Add all the ingredients and mix until well combined.

3. Preheat the oven to 175 degrees C and line the baking sheet with parchment paper.

4. Add a spoonful of the mixture until all the mixture is finished and spread it a little with the help of a spoon.

5. Bake the cookies for 12-15 minutes.

6. Serve immediately.

Nutrition Facts (per serving): Calories: 170, Carbohydrates: 30 g, Protein: 2 g, Fat: 8 g, Fiber: 4 g

12. Quinoa And Chia Seeds Energy Bites With Berries

Prep Time: 15 min	Cooking Time: 0min	Servings: 2

Ingredients:

- ¼ cup cooked quinoa
- 1 tbsp chia seeds
- 2 tbsp peanut butter
- ¼ cup dried blueberries
- 1 tbsp dried cranberries
- 1 tbsp manuka honey
- 1 tsp vanilla extract

Instructions:

1. Cook the quinoa as per package instructions.

2. Combine all the ingredients properly. If the mixture is too dry add 1 tbsp of coconut oil.

3. Shape this mixture into small round bites.

4. Refrigerate them for 1 hour so that they hold together properly.

5. Serve immediately.

Nutrition Facts (per serving): Calories: 170, Carbohydrates: 25 g, Protein: 25 g, Fat: 8 g, Fiber: 4 g

13. Healthy Fiber-Rich Fruits Salad Bowl

Prep Time: 10 min	Cooking Time: 0min	Servings: 1

Ingredients:

- ½ cup strawberries, halved
- ¼ cup fresh pineapple chunks
- 1 medium kiwi, sliced
- ¼ cup red grapes
- ¼ cup blueberries
- 5 g almonds, chopped
- 1 tsp granola

Instructions:

1. Combine all the ingredients in a bowl.

2. Add the chopped almonds and granola on top.

3. Serve immediately.

Nutrition Facts (per serving):

Calories: 120, Carbohydrates: 30 g, Protein: 2 g, Fat: 2 g, Fiber: 6 g

CHAPTER 9:
DRINKS TO FUEL YOUR DAY

1. Golden Turmeric Cinnamon-Infused Milk

Prep Time: 2 min	Cooking Time: 8 min	Servings: 1

Ingredients:

- 1 ½ cup almond or low-fat milk
- ¼ tsp turmeric powder
- 1 tsp manuka honey
- 1/8 tsp cinnamon powder
- Pinch of nutmeg powder

Instructions:

1. Boil the milk in a saucepan. Add the turmeric powder, cinnamon powder and nutmeg powder. Boil it for 5-7 minutes.

2. Strain the milk in a serving cup.

3. Add the manuka honey to it. Stir well.

4. Serve while warm.

Nutrition Facts (per serving):

Calories: 105, Carbohydrates: 18 g, Protein: 2 g, Fat: 4 g, Fiber: 2 g

2. Lemon and Ginger-infused Tea

Prep Time: 2 min	Cooking Time: 8 min	Servings: 1

Ingredients:

- 1 ½ cup spring water
- 1-inch piece of ginger, sliced
- 1 tbsp lemon juice
- Pinch of cinnamon powder
- 1 tsp manuka honey or stevia

Instructions:

1. Boil the water in a saucepan with the ginger, and cinnamon powder for 5-7 minutes.

2. Strain the tea in a serving cup.

3. Add manuka honey or stevia and lemon juice to it. Stir well.

4. Serve immediately.

Nutrition Facts (per serving):

Calories: 21, Carbohydrates: 6 g, Protein: 0 g, Fat: 0 g, Fiber: 0 g

3. Lemon-infused Rosemary Tea

Prep Time: 2 min	Cooking Time: 8 min	Servings: 1

Ingredients:

- 1 ½ cup spring water
- 1 tsp dried rosemary leaves
- 1 tbsp lime juice
- 1 tbsp raw honey or stevia
- Lemon slices (for garnish)

Instructions:

1. Boil the water in a saucepan with the rosemary leaves for 5-7 minutes.

2. Strain the tea in a serving cup.

3. Add the raw honey or stevia and lemon juice to it. Stir well.

4. Serve and garnish with lemon slices on top.

Nutrition Facts (per serving):

Calories: 21, Carbohydrates: 6 g, Protein: 0 g, Fat: 0 g, Fiber: 0 g

4. Mint-infused Fenugreek Seeds Tea

Prep Time: 2 min	Cooking Time: 8 min	Servings: 1

Ingredients:

- 1 ½ cup spring water
- 1/4 tsp fenugreek seeds
- Fresh mint leaves
- 1 tbsp raw honey or stevia
- Lemon slices (for garnish)

Instructions:

1. Boil the water in a saucepan with the fenugreek seeds for 5-7 minutes.

2. Strain the tea in a serving cup.

3. Add the raw honey or stevia and lemon juice to it. Stir well.

4. Serve and garnish with lemon slices on top.

Nutrition Facts (per serving):

Calories: 30, Carbohydrates: 6 g, Protein: 0 g, Fat: 0 g, Fiber: 0 g

5. Orange-Infused Oolong Iced Tea

Prep Time: 10 min	Cooking Time: 0 min	Servings: 1

Ingredients:

- 1 ½ cup spring water
- 1 tsp oolong tea leaves
- 1 tbsp orange juice
- 1 tbsp raw honey or stevia
- Orange slices (for garnish)
- Ice cubes as needed

Instructions:

1. Boil the water in a saucepan with the oolong tea leaves for 5-7 minutes.

2. Strain the tea in a serving glass.

3. Fill the glass with ice cubes and transfer the tea over it. Add the honey or stevia. Stir well.

4. Serve and place orange slices in it.

Nutrition Facts (per serving):

Calories: 31, Carbohydrates: 6 g, Protein: 0 g, Fat: 0 g, Fiber: 0 g

6. Lemon-infused Ginkgo Biloba Tea

Prep Time: 2 min	Cooking Time: 8 min	Servings: 1

Ingredients:

- 1 ½ cup spring water
- 1 tsp dried ginkgo biloba leaves
- Juice of 1 lime
- 1 tbsp raw honey or stevia
- Lemon slices (for garnish)

Instructions:

1. Boil the water in a saucepan with the dried ginkgo biloba leaves for 5-7 minutes.

2. Strain the tea in a serving cup.

3. Add the raw honey or stevia and lemon juice to it. Stir well.

4. Serve and garnish with lemon slices on top.

Nutrition Facts (per serving):

Calories: 31, Carbohydrates: 6 g, Protein: 0 g, Fat: 0 g, Fiber: 0 g

7. Energy Blast Strawberry Drink

Prep Time: 2 min	Cooking Time: 8 min	Servings: 1

Ingredients:

- ½ cup fresh or frozen strawberries
- ½ small banana
- 1 cup oat milk
- 1 tsp ashwagandha powder
- Pinch of cinnamon powder
- 3 Medjool dates
- Ice cubes as needed

Instructions:

1. Blend all the ingredients at high speed until you achieve a smooth and creamy consistency.

2. Serve immediately.

Nutrition Facts (per serving):

Calories: 211, Carbohydrates: 37 g, Protein: 4 g, Fat: 6 g, Fiber: 6.3 g

8. Mango Oats Smoothie

Prep Time: 2 min	Cooking Time: 8 min	Servings: 1

Ingredients:

- ½ cup fresh or frozen mango chunks
- ½ small banana
- 1 tbsp oats
- 1 cup almond milk
- ½ tsp flaxseeds
- Ice cubes as needed

Instructions:

1. Blend all the ingredients at high speed until you achieve a smooth and creamy consistency.

2. Serve immediately.

Nutrition Facts (per serving):

Calories: 171, Carbohydrates: 32 g, Protein: 4 g, Fat: 4.4 g, Fiber: 5.6 g

9. Pomegranate and Beet Drink

Prep Time:	Cooking Time: 0 min	Servings:
15 min		1

Ingredients:

- 1 cup pomegranate seeds
- 1 small beet, chopped
- ½ cup orange juice
- 1/2 cup sparkling water
- Pinch of sea salt and black pepper
- ¼ tsp ginseng powder
- Ice cubes as needed

Instructions:

1. Blend all the ingredients at high speed until you achieve the desired consistency.

2. Strain the drink in a serving glass.

3. Serve immediately.

Nutrition Facts (per serving):

Calories: 237, Carbohydrates: 53 g, Protein: 4.5 g, Fat: 2.3 g, Fiber: 9.75 g

10. Refreshing Lime and Cherry Drink

Prep Time:	Cooking Time: 0 min	Servings:
15 min		1

Ingredients:

- 1 cup cherries, pitted
- 1 cup sparkling water
- Pinch of sea salt and black pepper
- 1 tsp lime juice
- Ice cubes as needed

Instructions:

1. Blend all the ingredients at high speed until you achieve the desired consistency.

2. Strain the drink in a serving glass.

3. Serve immediately.

Nutrition Facts (per serving):

Calories: 98, Carbohydrates: 25 g, Protein: 1.6 g, Fat: 0.3 g, Fiber: 3.3 g

11. Green Booster Energy Drink

Prep Time:	Cooking Time: 0 min	Servings:
10 min		1

Ingredients:

- 1 cup baby spinach leave
- 1 small green apple
- ½ banana
- ½ cup almond milk or coconut water
- 1 tsp raw honey
- 1 tsp chia seeds

Instructions:

1. Blend all the ingredients at high speed until you achieve the desired consistency.

2. Transfer the drink to a serving glass.

3. Serve immediately.

Nutrition Facts (per serving):

Calories: 234, Carbohydrates: 46 g, Protein: 5.5 g, Fat: 5.3 g, Fiber: 2.7 g

12. Tropical Pineapple Energy Drink

Prep Time:	Cooking Time: 0 min	Servings:
10 min		1

Ingredients:

- 1 cup fresh or frozen pineapple chunks
- ½ small banana
- 1 cup coconut water
- 1 tsp flaxseeds
- ½ cup ice cubes

Instructions:

1. Blend all the ingredients at high speed until you achieve the desired consistency.

2. Transfer the drink to a serving glass.

3. Serve immediately.

Nutrition Facts (per serving):

Calories: 190, Carbohydrates: 43.2 g, Protein: 3.6 g, Fat: 2.2 g, Fiber: 7 g

13. Citrusy Peach Smoothie

Prep Time:	Cooking Time: 0 min	Servings:
10 min		1

Ingredients:

- 1 cup fresh or frozen peaches
- ¼ cup pineapple chunks
- 1 cup orange juice
- ¼ cup Greek yogurt
- 1 tbsp flaxseeds
- 1 tsp stevia

Instructions:

1. Blend all the ingredients at high speed until you achieve the desired consistency.

2. Transfer the drink in a serving glass.

3. Serve immediately.

Nutrition Facts (per serving):

Calories: 280, Carbohydrates: 58.2 g, Protein: 11.1 g, Fat: 5.5 g, Fiber: 5.8 g

CHAPTER 10:
DETOX MEALS TO BOOST METABOLISM

1. Green Broccoli Salad With Olives And Lime Dressing

Prep Time: 15 min	Cooking Time: 0min	Servings: 1

Ingredients:

- 1 cup broccoli florets, chopped
- 1 cup carrots, diced
- 1 cup lettuce, chopped
- 1 cup purple cabbage, chopped
- 2-3 green olives

For the dressing:

- 2 tbsp apple cider vinegar
- 1 tsp sesame seeds
- 1 tsp extra virgin olive oil
- Salt and black pepper as per taste

Instructions:

1. Combine all the ingredients in a bowl.

2. Mix the dressing ingredients and drizzle over the salad.

3. Serve immediately.

Nutrition Facts (per serving): Calories: 218, Carbohydrates: 35 g, Protein: 8 g, Fat: 8 g, Fiber: 11.5 g

2. Spinach Arugula Pear Salad With Walnuts

Prep Time: 15 min	Cooking Time: 0min	Servings: 1

Ingredients:

- 1 cup baby spinach leaves
- ½ cup arugula
- 1 large pear, sliced
- 5 g walnuts

For the dressing:

- 2 tbsp balsamic vinegar
- 1 tbsp avocado oil
- 1 tsp raw honey

Instructions:

1. Combine all the ingredients in a bowl.

2. Mix the dressing ingredients and drizzle over the salad.

3. Serve immediately.

Nutrition Facts (per serving): Calories: 313, Carbohydrates: 41.2 g, Protein: 3.7 g, Fat: 17.7 g, Fiber: 6.8 g

3. Citrusy Detox Green Smoothie

Prep Time:	Cooking Time: 0min	Servings:
10 min		1

Ingredients:

- 1 cup baby spinach leaves
- 50 g avocado, chopped
- 1 large orange, freshly squeezed
- 1 cup sparkling water
- 1 tbsp lime juice
- 1 tsp avocado honey
- ½ tsp moringa powder

Instructions:

1. Combine all the ingredients in a blender.

2. Blend at high speed until you achieve the desired consistency.

3. Transfer the smoothie into a glass and garnish it with a slice of orange on top.

3. Serve immediately.

Nutrition Facts (per serving): Calories: 180, Carbohydrates: 28.3 g, Protein: 4 g, Fat: 7.8 g, Fiber: 4.8 g

4. Lime-Infused Chickpea Mint Avocado Bowl

Prep Time:	Cooking Time: 0min	Servings:
15 min		1

Ingredients:

- 1 cup chickpeas, drained and rinsed
- 50 g avocado, chopped
- 1 medium cucumber, chopped

For the dressing:

- ¼ cup low-fat yogurt
- ¼ cup mint leaves, chopped
- 1 tsp lime juice
- 1 tsp extra virgin olive oil
- Salt and black pepper as per taste

Instructions:

1. Combine all the ingredients in a bowl.

2. Mix the dressing ingredients (low-fat yogurt, mint leaves, olive oil, salt, pepper, and balsamic vinegar), and set it aside.

3. Add the dressing over the chickpeas, chopped avocado and cucumber.

4. Serve immediately.

Nutrition Facts (per serving): Calories: 401, Carbohydrates: 51.9 g, Protein: 16.4 g, Fat: 16.1 g, Fiber: 14.8 g

5. Whole Wheat Quinoa Wrap With Asparagus And Beans

Prep Time: 12 min	Cooking Time: 2 min	Servings: 1

Ingredients:

- 1 whole wheat tortilla
- ¼ cup cooked quinoa of any preferred brand
- 2 asparagus spears, trimmed and chopped
- ¼ cup black beans, canned
- 1 plum tomato, chopped
- 1 cucumber, chopped
- 50 g avocado, chopped

For the sauce:

- 2 tbsp tahini
- 1 tbsp lime juice
- 1/8 tsp garlic powder
- 1 tsp extra virgin olive oil

Instructions:

1. Mix the sauce ingredients and set them aside.

2. Slightly toast the tortilla on a pan over medium heat. Place the whole wheat tortilla wrap over a flat surface. Add the cooked quinoa, chopped tomato, cucumber, asparagus, and black beans.

3. Add the prepared sauce over it. Roll it over in the form of a wrap.

4. Serve immediately.

Nutrition Facts (per serving): Calories: 562, Carbohydrates: 58.6 g, Protein: 18 g, Fat: 35 g, Fiber: 14.8 g

6. Green Detox Smoothie

Prep Time: 8 min	Cooking Time: 0 min	Servings: 1

Ingredients:

- 1 medium green apple, chopped
- 1 celery stalk, chopped
- 1 medium cucumber, chopped
- 1 tbsp lime juice
- 1 cup sparkling water
- ½ tsp ginseng powder
- 1 tsp avocado honey
- ½ cup ice cubes

Instructions:

1. Combine all the ingredients in a blender.

2. Blend at high speed until you achieve the desired consistency.

3. Transfer the smoothie into a serving glass and garnish with a slice of lemon on top.

4. Serve immediately.

Nutrition Facts (per serving): Calories: 147, Carbohydrates: 38.2 g, Protein: 2 g, Fat: 0.6 g, Fiber: 6.05 g

2. Mix the dressing ingredients and drizzle over the salad.

3. Serve immediately.

Nutrition Facts (per serving): Calories: 324, Carbohydrates: 70.7 g, Protein: 4.6 g, Fat: 13.6 g, Fiber: 6.1 g

7. Orange Arugula Pecan Salad With Balsamic Vinegar Dressing

Prep Time: 15 min	Cooking Time: 0 min	Servings: 1

Ingredients:

- 2 large Valencia oranges, peeled and segmented
- ½ cup arugula
- ½ cup baby spinach leaves
- 5 g pecans
- 1 medium Fuji apple, sliced
- 1 tsp poppy seeds

For the dressing:

- 2 tbsp balsamic vinegar
- 1 tsp raw honey

Instructions:

1. Combine all the ingredients in a bowl.

8. Cauliflower Kale Chickpea Bowl With Parsley

Prep Time: 15 min	Cooking Time: 3 min	Servings: 1

Ingredients:

- 1 cup cauliflower florets
- ½ cup chickpeas, canned
- ¼ cup baby kale leaves
- 1 tbsp parsley
- 1 tbsp lime juice
- Salt and pepper as per taste

Instructions:

1. Sauté the cauliflower florets, and chickpeas in a non-stick pan for 2-3 minutes.

2. Transfer them to a bowl and add the baby kale leaves, lime juice, pepper, and parsley. Mix well.

3. Serve immediately.

Nutrition Facts (per serving): Calories: 120, Carbohydrates: 23 g, Protein: 5.5 g, Fat: 2.2 g, Fiber: 7.3 g

9. Spinach Beet Quinoa Detox Salad

Prep Time:	Cooking Time: 0min	Servings:
15 min		1

Ingredients:

- ½ cup cooked quinoa
- 1 medium beet, chopped
- ½ cup pomegranate seeds
- ½ cup baby spinach leaves
- 1 tbsp lime juice
- Salt and pepper as per taste

Instructions:

1. Combine all the ingredients in a bowl. Mix well.

2. Serve immediately.

Nutrition Facts (per serving): Calories: 263, Carbohydrates: 47.5 g, Protein: 8.1 g, Fat: 4.2 g, Fiber: 8.6 g

10. Zucchini Basil-Infused Soup

Prep Time:	Cooking Time: 15 min	2w`
10 min		

Ingredients:

- 1 tbsp extra virgin olive oil
- 2 medium zucchinis
- 1 medium onion, chopped
- 3 cups of vegetable broth
- 1-2 cloves of garlic
- ¼ tsp red chilli flakes
- 1 tsp balsamic vinegar
- ¼ cup basil leaves
- Salt and black pepper as per taste

Instructions:

1. Combine all the ingredients in a saucepan and cook over medium heat. Cook for 10-15 minutes.

2. Transfer this mixture to a blender and blend until you achieve a smooth and creamy consistency.

3. Serve immediately and garnish with fresh cilantro leaves on top.

Nutrition Facts (per serving): Calories: 174, Carbohydrates: 20.2 g, Protein: 3.5 g, Fat: 11.3 g, Fiber: 4.5 g

11. Cranberry Detox Mint Juice

Prep Time:	Cooking Time: 0min	Servings:
7 min		1

Ingredients:

- ½ cup cranberries
- ¼ cup mint leaves
- 1 tbsp lime juice
- 1 tsp stevia
- Ice cubes as needed

Instructions:

1. Combine all the ingredients in a blender.

2. Blend at high speed until you achieve the desired consistency.

3. Transfer the juice to a glass and garnish with mint leaves.

4. Serve immediately.

Nutrition Facts (per serving): Calories: 61, Carbohydrates: 16.2 g, Protein: 2.6 g, Fat: 0.7 g, Fiber: 2.6 g

12. Broccoli And Zucchini Salad with Olive Oil Dill Dressing

Prep Time:	Cooking Time: 0min	Servings:
12 min		1

Ingredients:

- 1 cup zucchini, chopped
- 1 medium cucumber, chopped
- 1 cup cherry tomatoes, chopped
- ½ cup broccoli florets
- Fresh cilantro leaves

For the dressing:

- 1 tbsp avocado oil
- 1 tbsp lime juice
- ¼ tsp dill

Instructions:

1. Combine all the ingredients in a bowl.

2. Prepare the dressing and drizzle it over the bowl.

3. Serve immediately and garnish with fresh cilantro leaves on top.

Nutrition Facts (per serving): Calories: 146, Carbohydrates: 17.5 g, Protein: 4.5 g, Fat: 10.5 g, Fiber: 6.5 g

13. Blackberry Arugula Salad with Cashews

Prep Time:	Cooking Time: 0min	Servings:
10 min		1

Ingredients:

- 1 cup fresh blackberries
- ½ cup arugula
- 1 cup Fuji apple, chopped
- ½ cup red cabbage
- 5 g cashews

For the dressing:

- 1 tbsp avocado oil
- 1 tbsp lime juice
- 1 tbsp raw honey

Instructions:

1. Combine all the ingredients in a bowl.

2. Prepare the dressing and drizzle it over the bowl.

3. Serve immediately and garnish with cashews on top.

Nutrition Facts (per serving): Calories: 242, Carbohydrates: 34.5 g, Protein: 4.5 g, Fat: 17 g, Fiber:

8-WEEK MEAL PLAN

Week 1

Days	Breakfast	Lunch	Dinner
Day 1	Scrambled eggs and veggie breakfast bowl	Green Spinach Pasta with creamy parmesan sauce	Chicken Zucchini Frittata Casserole
Day 2	Quinoa High-Protein Breakfast Bowl	Grilled Turkey and veggie wrap + Quinoa Black Bean Salad with Lime dressing	Greek Turkey Lettuce Rolls
Day 3	Cauliflower Kale Chickpea Bowl with Parsley + Blueberry Banana Smoothie	Peach and avocado salad with feta cheese topping + Zucchini Basil-Infused Soup	Blackberry Arugula Salad with Cashews + Grilled Mahi-Mahi with Mango Salsa
Day 4	Almond yogurt parfait with assorted fruits	Crunchy Strawberry Spinach Salad + Cranberry Detox Mint Juice	Turkey Meatballs with Zucchini Noodles
Day 5	Oatmeal Breakfast Bowl	Whole wheat Tuna wrap + Orange Arugula Pecan Salad with balsamic vinegar dressing	Slow-Cooked Lemon Basil Chicken
Day 6	Overnight Chia Seeds Breakfast Bowl + Green Detox Smoothie	Garlic Salmon Patties with coleslaw salad	Slow-cooked Chicken Fajitas
Day 7	Strawberry Almond Oats Smoothie + Hard Boiled Eggs Veggie Salad	Blueberry and arugula salad with Cheese	Chicken Zucchini Frittata Casserole

Week 2

Day 1	Muesli and Oatmeal Waffle with Apricots	Crunchy Strawberry Spinach Salad + Zucchini Basil-Infused Soup	Eggplant and Chickpea Stew
Day 2	Almond yogurt parfait with assorted fruits	Mixed Beans and Veggie Salad + Whole Wheat Quinoa Wrap with Asparagus and Beans	Moroccan Lamb with Cauliflower Rice
Day 3	Scrambled eggs and veggie breakfast bowl	Blackberry Arugula Salad with Cashews + Grilled chicken breast with avocado and pomegranate seeds	Greek Turkey Lettuce Rolls + Slow-cooked Chicken Fajitas
Day 4	Strawberry Smoothie Bowl with nuts and granola	Sesame Chicken with sauteed veggies	Grilled Tofu and Quinoa Bowl + Green Broccoli Salad with Olives and Lime Dressing
Day 5	Cinnamon Sweet Potato Oatmeal Pancakes + Overnight Oatmeal high-fiber breakfast	Edamame Beans Cucumber Kale Salad	Slow-cooked barbecue Chicken + Spinach Beet Quinoa Detox Salad
Day 6	Mixed Berries Smoothie Fusion + Quinoa High-Protein Breakfast Bowl	Grilled Turkey and veggie wrap	Chicken Zucchini Frittata Casserole
Day 7	Hard Boiled Eggs Veggie Salad + Creamy Spinach and Pear Smoothie	Broccoli Veggie Pasta Salad with pine nuts	Grilled Mahi-Mahi with Mango Salsa

Week 3

Day 1	Oatmeal Breakfast Bowl + Zucchini Basil-Infused Soup	Green Spinach Pasta with creamy parmesan sauce	Eggplant and Chickpea Stew
Day 2	Green Avocado Smoothie + Cauliflower Kale Chickpea Bowl with Parsley	Quinoa Black Bean Salad with Lime dressing	Herbed Chicken Thighs with Cauliflower Mash
Day 3	Overnight Oatmeal high-fiber breakfast	Whole wheat Tuna wrap + Mixed Beans and Veggie Salad	Slow-Cooked Lemon Basil Chicken
Day 4	Scrambled eggs and veggie breakfast bowl + Almond yogurt parfait with assorted fruits	Crunchy Strawberry Spinach Salad + Green Detox Smoothie	Grilled Mahi-Mahi with Mango Salsa
Day 5	Hard Boiled Eggs Veggie Salad	Green Spinach Pasta with creamy parmesan sauce	Grilled Tofu and Quinoa Bowl
Day 6	Cinnamon Sweet Potato Oatmeal Pancakes + Spinach Beet Quinoa Detox Salad	Broccoli Veggie Pasta Salad with pine nuts	Turkey Meatballs with Zucchini Noodles
Day 7	Strawberry Almond Oats Smoothie + Broccoli and zucchini Salad with Olive Oil Dill dressing	Whole wheat Tuna wrap	Chicken Zucchini Frittata Casserole

Week 4

Day 1	Almond yogurt parfait with assorted fruits	Blueberry and arugula salad with Cheese	Moroccan Lamb with Cauliflower Rice
Day 2	Creamy Spinach and Pear Smoothie + Quinoa High-Protein Breakfast Bowl	Grilled Turkey and veggie wrap	Cooked Chicken Fajitas
Day 3	Overnight Oatmeal high-fiber breakfast	Blueberry and arugula salad with Cheese + Whole wheat Tuna wrap	Eggplant and Chickpea Stew
Day 4	Overnight Chia Seeds Breakfast Bowl	Quinoa Black Bean Salad with Lime dressing	Slow-Cooked Lemon Basil Chicken
Day 5	Scrambled eggs and veggie breakfast bowl	Mixed Beans and Veggie Salad	Turkey Meatballs with Zucchini Noodles
Day 6	Almond yogurt parfait with assorted fruits	Peach and avocado salad with feta cheese topping	Grilled Tofu and Quinoa Bowl + Eggplant and Chickpea Stew
Day 7	Muesli and Oatmeal Waffle with Apricots	Green Spinach Pasta with creamy parmesan sauce	Herbed Chicken Thighs with Cauliflower Mash

Week 5

Day 1	Scrambled eggs and veggie breakfast bowl + Oatmeal Breakfast Bowl	Grilled Turkey and veggie wrap	Eggplant and Chickpea Stew
Day 2	Overnight Oatmeal high-fiber breakfast	Quinoa Black Bean Salad with Lime dressing	Slow-cooked Chicken Fajitas
Day 3	Almond yogurt parfait with assorted fruits	Garlic Salmon Patties with coleslaw salad	Grilled Tofu and Quinoa Bowl
Day 4	Mixed Berries Smoothie Fusion + Overnight Chia seeds Breakfast Bowl	Whole wheat Tuna wrap	Greek Turkey Lettuce Rolls+ Blackberry Arugula Salad with Cashews
Day 5	Broccoli and zucchini Salad with Olive Oil Dill dressing	Peach and avocado salad with feta cheese topping	Chicken Zucchini Frittata Casserole
Day 6	Oatmeal Breakfast Bowl	Grilled Turkey and veggie wrap	Grilled Mahi-Mahi with Mango Salsa
Day 7	Cinnamon Sweet Potato Oatmeal Pancakes	Crunchy Strawberry Spinach Salad	Seared Scallops with Spinach

Week 6

Day 1	Scrambled eggs and veggie breakfast bowl	Quinoa Black Bean Salad with Lime dressing	Moroccan Lamb with Cauliflower Rice
Day 2	Creamy Spinach and Pear Smoothie + Oatmeal Breakfast Bowl	Blueberry and arugula salad with Cheese	Herbed Chicken Thighs with Cauliflower Mash
Day 3	Orange Arugula Pecan Salad with balsamic vinegar dressing	Whole Wheat Quinoa Wrap with Asparagus and Beans	Slow-Cooked Lemon Basil Chicken
Day 4	Quinoa High-Protein Breakfast Bowl	Broccoli Veggie Pasta Salad with pine nuts	Chicken Zucchini Frittata Casserole
Day 5	Zucchini Basil-Infused Soup + Spinach Beet Quinoa Detox Salad	Garlic Salmon Patties with coleslaw salad	Slow-cooked Chicken Fajitas
Day 6	Overnight Oatmeal high-fiber breakfast	Grilled chicken breast with avocado and pomegranate seeds	Eggplant and Chickpea Stew
Day 7	Mixed Berries Smoothie Fusion + Overnight Chia seeds Breakfast Bowl	Quinoa Black Bean Salad with Lime dressing	Chicken Zucchini Frittata Casserole

Week 7

Day 1	Blueberry Banana Smoothie	Green Spinach Pasta with creamy parmesan sauce	Slow-Cooked Barbecue Chicken
Day 2	Muesli and Oatmeal Waffle with Apricots	Mixed Beans and Veggie Salad + Grilled Turkey and veggie wrap	Slow-Cooked Lemon Basil Chicken
Day 3	Green Avocado Smoothie + Scrambled eggs and veggie breakfast bowl	Whole Wheat Quinoa Wrap with Asparagus and Beans	Seared Scallops with Spinach
Day 4	Orange Arugula Pecan Salad with balsamic vinegar dressing	Quinoa Black Bean Salad with Lime dressing	Grilled Mahi-Mahi with Mango Salsa
Day 5	Almond yogurt parfait with assorted fruits	Sesame Chicken with sauteed veggies	Turkey Meatballs with Zucchini Noodles
Day 6	Overnight Oatmeal high-fiber breakfast	Peach and avocado salad with feta cheese topping	Eggplant and Chickpea Stew
Day 7	Broccoli and zucchini Salad with Olive Oil Dill dressing + Creamy Spinach and Pear Smoothie	Mixed Beans and Veggie Salad	Greek Turkey Lettuce Rolls

Week 8

Day 1	Quinoa High-Protein Breakfast Bowl	Green Spinach Pasta with creamy parmesan sauce	Slow-Cooked Lemon Basil Chicken
Day 2	Strawberry Smoothie Bowl with nuts and granola	Peach and avocado salad with feta cheese topping	Grilled Tofu and Quinoa Bowl
Day 3	Overnight Chia Seeds Breakfast Bowl	Grilled chicken breast with avocado and pomegranate seeds	Moroccan Lamb with Cauliflower Rice
Day 4	Lime-infused Chickpea Mint Avocado Bowl + Hard Boiled Eggs Veggie Salad	Blueberry and arugula salad with Cheese	Avocado Tuna Salad + Turkey Meatballs with Zucchini Noodles
Day 5	Strawberry Almond Oats Smoothie + Scrambled eggs and veggie breakfast bowl	Crunchy Strawberry Spinach Salad	Slow-Cooked Barbecue Chicken
Day 6	Mixed Berries Smoothie Fusion	Peach and avocado salad with feta cheese topping	Grilled Mahi-Mahi with Mango Salsa
Day 7	Oatmeal Breakfast Bowl + Almond yogurt parfait with assorted fruits	Blueberry and arugula salad with Cheese	Greek Turkey Lettuce Rolls

GROCERY LIST

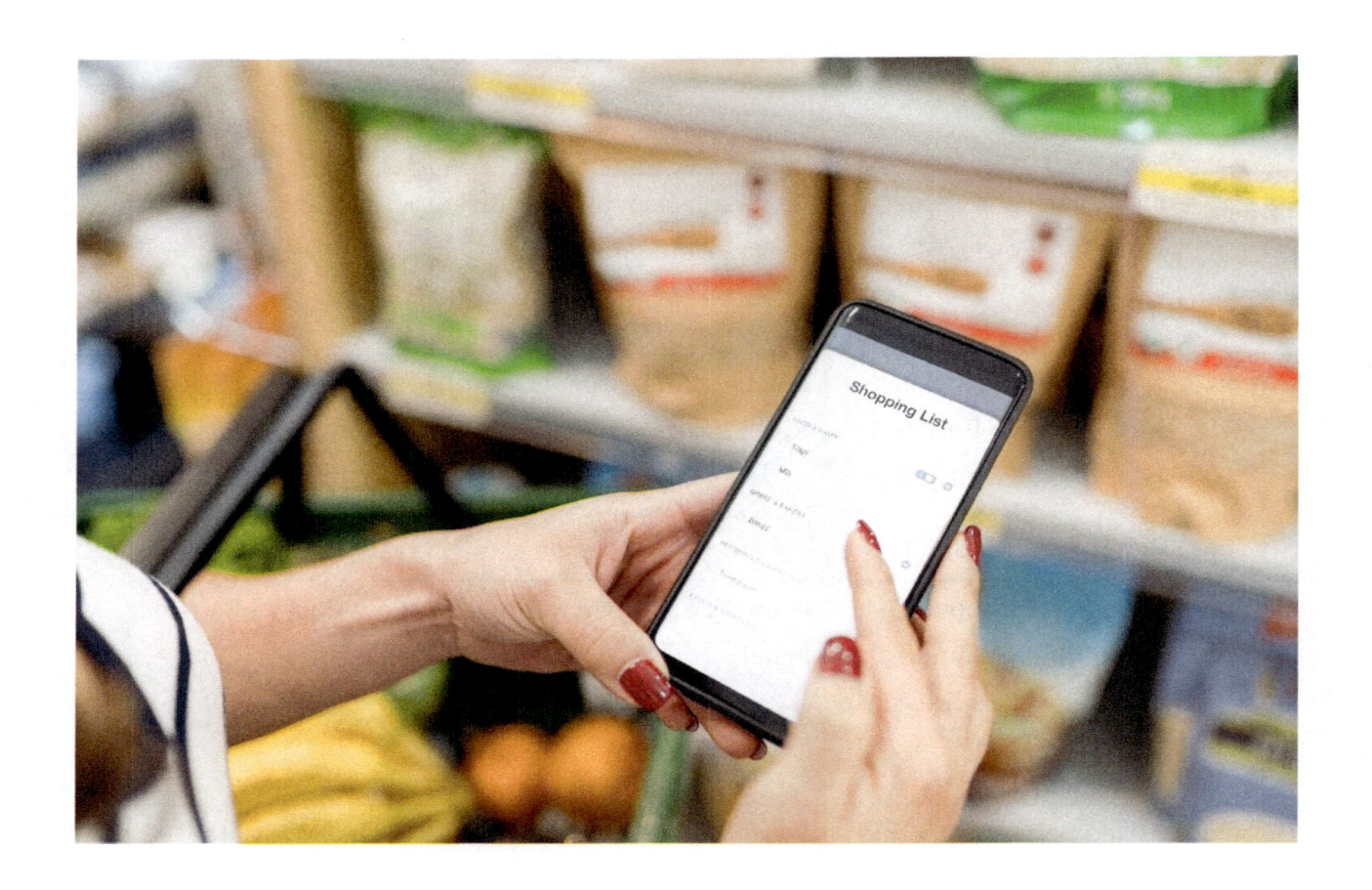

Week 1

Fruits and Vegetables

- Fresh baby spinach leaves: 2 cups (1 cup + ½ cup)
- Cherry tomatoes: 1 cup
- Red bell pepper: ½ cup
- Broccoli florets: ¼ cup
- Zucchini: 3 medium
- Onions (red and yellow): 2 medium
- Garlic: 4-5 cloves
- Fresh or frozen peaches: 1 cup
- Avocado: 2 medium
- Mango: 1 medium
- Cucumber: 1 medium
- Fresh lettuce leaves: As needed
- Arugula: ½ cup
- Fuji apple: 1 medium
- Mixed berries (blueberries, strawberries, raspberries): 1 cup each
- Banana: 1 small
- Medjool dates: 7-8
- Grated carrot: ¼ cup
- Red cabbage: ½ cup
- Green cabbage: ½ cup
- Cilantro: A handful (for garnish)
- Basil leaves: ¼ cup
- Fresh parsley: 2 tablespoons
- Fresh mint leaves: ¼ cup
- Lemon: 1 (for juice)
- Lime: 3 (for juice)
- Orange: 2 large
- Cauliflower florets: 1 cup
- Baby kale leaves: ¼ cup
- Green onions: 1 bunch
- Fresh or frozen blackberries: 1 cup

Proteins

- Medium eggs: 2

- Chicken breasts: 3 pieces (about 1.5 lbs total)
- Ground turkey breast: 100 g
- Mahi-mahi fillet: 1 fillet
- Canned tuna: 1 can
- Canned salmon: 1 can
- Greek yogurt: 1.5 cups (½ cup + ¼ cup + ½ cup)
- Feta cheese: ½ cup
- Mozzarella cheese: ¼ cup
- Cheddar cheese: 2 tablespoons
- Parmesan cheese: ¾ cup (¼ cup + 2 tablespoons + 3 tablespoons)

Seeds and Nuts

- Walnuts: 10 g (about ¼ cup)
- Pecans: 5 g (about 2 tablespoons)
- Almonds: 15 g (about ¼ cup)
- Brazil nuts: 5 g (about 2 tablespoons)
- Cashews: 5 g (about 2 tablespoons)
- Flaxseeds: 2 tablespoons
- Chia seeds: 3 tablespoons (1 tablespoon + 2 teaspoons)
- Sunflower seeds: ¼ cup
- Pumpkin seeds: ¼ cup

Cereals and Starches

- Whole wheat pasta: 1 cup
- Whole wheat tortilla wraps: 2
- Cooked quinoa: 1 cup (or ¼ cup dry)
- Rolled oats: ¾ cup (½ cup + 2 tablespoons)
- Muesli: ¼ cup
- Breadcrumbs: ¼ cup

Herbs, Condiments, Spices, and Oils

- Extra virgin olive oil: 5 tablespoons (1 tsp + 1 tbsp + 1 tbsp + 1 tbsp + 1 tbsp)
- Avocado oil: 1 tablespoon
- Balsamic vinegar: 3 tablespoons (1 tbsp + 1 tbsp + 1 tsp)
- Dijon mustard: 1 tablespoon
- Light mayonnaise: 4 tablespoons (2 tbsp + 2 tbsp)
- Honey (acacia or raw): 4 tablespoons (1 tbsp + 1 tbsp + 1 tbsp + 1 tbsp)
- Stevia: 1 tsp

- Ginger-garlic paste: 1 tablespoon
- Dried oregano: 1 teaspoon
- Dried thyme: 1 teaspoon
- Paprika powder: ¼ teaspoon
- Red chili flakes: ¼ teaspoon
- Sea salt: To taste
- Black pepper: To taste
- Garlic powder: 1 teaspoon
- Ground cinnamon: ½ teaspoon
- Cardamom powder: Pinch
- Ginseng powder: ½ teaspoon
- Sesame seeds: 1 teaspoon
- Manuka honey: 1 tablespoon (for drizzling)

Week 2

Fruits and Vegetables

- Strawberries: 2 cups (1 cup halved + ¼ cup halved + ½ cup halved)
- Blueberries: 1.25 cups (½ cup + ¼ cup + ½ cup)
- Raspberries: 1.5 cups (½ cup + ½ cup + ½ cup)
- Kiwis: 3 (2 peeled and cubed + 1 sliced)
- Bananas: 3 (1 small diced + ½ small diced + 1 large mashed)
- Mango: 1 medium diced
- Apple (Fuji): 2 medium (1 chopped + ½ diced)
- Pear: 1 medium chopped
- Zucchini: 3 medium (2 chopped + 1 sliced)
- Eggplant: ½ medium, diced
- Cucumbers: 3 medium (1 chopped + 1 diced + 1 chopped)
- Tomatoes: 3 medium (1 diced + ½ cup chopped + ½ cup sliced)
- Red bell pepper: ¼ cup
- Broccoli florets: 2.5 cups (¼ cup + 1 cup chopped + 1 cup chopped)
- Carrots: 1 cup diced
- Onion: 2.5 medium (1 chopped + ½ chopped + ½ sliced + ¼ cup red onion)
- Garlic: 6-7 cloves
- Baby spinach leaves: 2 cups (½ cup + 1 cup + ½ cup)
- Lettuce leaves: 1 cup chopped

- Arugula: ¼ cup
- Red cabbage: ½ cup
- Purple cabbage: 1 cup
- Brussels sprouts: ½ cup chopped
- Asparagus: 2 spears
- Pomegranate seeds: 1 cup (½ cup + ½ cup)
- Peas (canned): ½ cup
- Chili flakes: ¼ tsp
- Cilantro: A handful (for garnish)

Proteins
- Medium eggs: 4
- Chicken breasts: 3 (1 large + 2 medium)
- Ground turkey breast: 100 g
- Lamb chop: 1
- Mahi-mahi fillet: 1
- Canned chickpeas: 1.5 cups (½ cup + 1 cup)
- Canned kidney beans (red and white): 1 cup (½ cup each)
- Almond yogurt: ¼ cup
- Low-fat yogurt: ⅛ cup
- Goat cheese: ¼ cup
- Feta cheese: ¼ cup
- Mozzarella cheese: ¼ cup
- Cheddar cheese: 2 tablespoons

Seeds and Nuts
- Hazelnuts: 5 g
- Walnuts: 15 g (5 g + 5 g + 5 g)
- Almonds: 15 g (5 g + 5 g + 5 g)
- Brazil nuts: 10 g (5 g + 5 g)
- Cashews: 5 g
- Pine nuts: 5 g
- Flaxseeds: 2 tablespoons (1 tablespoon + 1 tsp)
- Chia seeds: 3 teaspoons (2 tsp soaked + 1 tsp)
- Hemp seeds: 3 tablespoons (2 tbsp + 1 tsp)
- Sesame seeds: 4 teaspoons (1 tsp + 1 tsp + 1 tsp + 1 tbsp)

Cereals and Starches
- Oat flour: 1 cup
- Rolled oats: 2.5 cups (1 cup + ¼ cup + ¼ cup + ¼ cup)
- Muesli: ½ cup (plus an additional 1 tbsp)
- Whole wheat tortillas: 2
- Cooked quinoa: 1.5 cups (½ cup + 1 cup)
- Sweet potato puree: 1 cup
- Rice (brown or white): 1 cup

Herbs, Condiments, Spices, and Oils
- Extra virgin olive oil: 5 tablespoons (1 tbsp + 1 tbsp + 1 tbsp + 1 tbsp + 1 tsp)
- Olive oil: 4 tablespoons (1 tbsp + 1 tbsp + 1 tbsp + 1 tbsp)
- Balsamic vinegar: 3 tablespoons (1 tsp + 1 tbsp + 1 tbsp)
- Tahini: 2 tablespoons
- Raw honey: 4 tablespoons (1 tbsp + 2 tbsp + 1 tbsp)
- Manuka honey: 2 tablespoons (1 tbsp + 1 tbsp)
- Soy sauce: 1 tablespoon
- Worcestershire sauce: 1 tablespoon
- Sesame oil: 1 tablespoon
- Lime juice: 5 tablespoons (1 tbsp + 1 tbsp + 1 tbsp + 1 tbsp + juice of 1 lime)
- Vanilla extract: 2 teaspoons (1 tsp + 1 tsp)
- Ground cinnamon: 1.5 teaspoons (½ tsp + ½ tsp + ½ tsp)
- Nutmeg powder: ¼ teaspoon
- Cumin powder: 2 teaspoons (½ tsp + 1 tsp)
- Paprika powder: 1.25 teaspoons (1 tsp + ¼ tsp + ¼ tsp)
- Red chili powder: 1 teaspoon
- Cayenne pepper: ¼ teaspoon
- Sea salt: To taste
- Black pepper: To taste
- Garlic powder: 1 teaspoon
- Cardamom powder: Pinch
- Dried oregano: 1 teaspoon

WEEK 3

Fruits and Vegetables
- Fresh raspberries: ½ cup

- Blueberries: ¼ cup
- Dried cranberries: ¼ cup
- Granny Smith apple: 1 small
- Avocado, chopped: 1 cup (½ cup x2)
- Fresh mango chunks: ½ cup
- Pineapple chunks: ¼ cup
- Beet, chopped: 1 medium
- Pomegranate seeds: ½ cup
- Strawberries, halved: 1 cup (½ cup x2)
- Banana, diced: 1 small (½ banana x3)
- Kiwis, peeled and cubed: 2
- Fresh or frozen peaches: ½ cup
- Green apple, chopped: 1 medium
- Cherry tomatoes, chopped: 1 cup (½ cup x2)
- Cucumber, chopped: 1 medium (½ cup x3)
- Tomato, chopped: 1 small (¼ cup x3)
- Zucchini: 3 medium (2 whole + 1 chopped)
- Eggplant, diced: ½
- Cauliflower florets: 1 cup
- Cauliflower: ½ head
- Baby spinach leaves: 3 ½ cups (1 cup x3 + ½ cup)
- Basil leaves: ¼ cup
- Baby kale leaves: 1 cup (½ cup x2)
- Cooked chickpeas: 1 ½ cups (½ cup x3)
- Black beans, rinsed: ½ cup
- Chopped onion: 1 ½ cups (1 small x2 + ½ cup)
- Broccoli florets: 1 cup (½ cup x2)
- Arugula: ¼ cup
- Celery stalk, chopped: 1
- Red bell pepper: ¼ cup
- Red onions: ¼ cup

Proteins
- Cooked tuna: 1 can
- Eggs: 4 medium (2 eggs x2)
- Skinless chicken thighs: 2

- Chicken breast: 1
- Ground turkey: 100 g
- Cooked quinoa: 2 1/2 cups (½ cup x5)
- Tofu: ½
- Whole egg: 1

Seeds and Nuts

- Walnuts: 25 g (5 g x5)
- Almonds, chopped: 15 g (5 g x3)
- Pecans, crushed: 5 g
- Brazil nuts: 5 g
- Pine nuts: 5 g
- Chia seeds: 3 tbsp (1 tbsp x3)
- Flaxseeds: 1 tsp
- Pumpkin seeds: 2 tbsp
- Hemp seeds: 3 tsp (1 tsp x3)
- Sunflower seeds: 1 tsp

Cereals and Starches

- Rolled oats: 1 ½ cups (½ cup x3)
- Oats: 1 ¼ cups (¼ cup x5)
- Whole wheat pasta: 2 cups (1 cup x2)
- Muesli: 3 tbsp (1 tbsp x3)
- Sweet potato puree: 1 cup
- Whole wheat tortilla wrap: 2
- Granola: ½ cup (¼ cup x2)

Herbs, Spices, Condiments, and Oils

- Extra virgin olive oil: 5 tbsp (1 tbsp x5)
- Unsalted butter: 6 tbsp (2 tbsp x3)
- Manuka honey: 3 tsp (1 tsp x3)
- Olive oil: 4 tbsp (1 tbsp x4)
- Lime juice: 7 tsp (1 tsp x6 + 1 tbsp)
- Lemon juice: 1 tbsp
- Red chili flakes: ¼ tsp
- Balsamic vinegar: 1 tbsp
- Dried oregano: ¼ tsp
- Parsley: ¼ tsp

- Black pepper: 1 ¼ tsp (¼ tsp x5)
- Salt: to taste
- Garlic powder: 1 tsp
- Ginger-garlic paste: 1 tbsp
- Greek yogurt: ¼ cup
- Light mayonnaise: 2 tbsp
- Almond butter: 3 tbsp (1 tbsp x3)
- Raw honey: 3 tbsp (1 tbsp x3)
- Dark chocolate chips: 1 tsp
- Ginseng powder: ½ tsp
- Avocado honey: 1 tsp
- Coconut oil: 1 tbsp

WEEK 4

Fruits and Vegetables
- Raspberries: 1 cup (½ cup x2)
- Blueberries: 1 ¾ cups (½ cup + ¼ cup + 1 cup)
- Kiwis: 3 (2 peeled and cubed + 1 sliced)
- Strawberries, sliced: 1 cup (½ cup x2)
- Apples: 2 small (1 sliced x2)
- Arugula: 1 cup (½ cup x2)
- Parmesan or feta cheese: 1 cup (½ cup x2)
- Garlic: 3 cloves (1 minced + 2 whole)
- Grated ginger: 1 tsp
- Bell peppers: ¾ cup (¼ cup red or yellow + ½ sliced)
- Baby spinach leaves: 1 ½ cups (½ cup + 1 cup)
- Pear: 1 medium, chopped
- Banana: ½ small (sliced) + ½ (sliced)
- Cucumber: 2 cups (½ cup + 1 cup)
- Cherry tomatoes: 1 ¼ cups (¼ cup + 1 cup)
- Broccoli florets: ¾ cup (½ cup + ¼ cup)
- Eggplant: 1 (½ diced x2)
- Mixed veggies: ½ cup (broccoli, carrot, bell peppers)
- Fresh lettuce leaves: 2 cups (1 cup + ½ cup chopped)
- Zucchini: 2 ½ cups (1 spiralized + ½ chopped + 1 chopped)

- Cauliflower rice: ½ cup
- Cauliflower: ½ head
- Cooked quinoa: 1 ½ cups (½ cup + ¼ cup + ½ cup)
- Mixed berries: ¼ cup
- Pomegranate seeds: ¼ cup
- Fresh cilantro leaves: 5 (Few leaves x2)
- Fresh basil: 1 bunch
- Fresh mango chunks: ½ cup
- Pineapple chunks: ¼ cup
- Peaches: 2 large, sliced or chopped
- Apricots: ½ cup
- Grapes, red: ¼ cup

Proteins
- Lamb chop: 1
- Chicken breasts: 2
- Skinless chicken thighs: 2
- Ground turkey: 100 g
- Canned chickpeas: 3 ½ cups (1 cup + ½ cup + ½ cup + 1 cup + ¼ cup)
- Canned tuna: 1 can
- Eggs: 3 medium (2 + 1)
- Tofu: ½
- Cooked turkey breast: 3 slices

Seeds and Nuts
- Chia seeds: 3 tbsp (2 tsp + 1 tbsp)
- Walnuts: 25 g (5 g x5)
- Pecans: 10 g (5 g x2)
- Almonds: 35 g (5 g x7)
- Mixed nuts: 3 tbsp (1 tbsp x3)
- Pumpkin seeds: 2 tbsp
- Hazelnuts: 5 g
- Medjool dates: 5 g
- Flax seeds: 3 tsp (1 tsp x3)
- Sesame seeds: 1 tsp

Cereals and Starches
- Rolled oats: 2 ¼ cups (1 cup + 2 tbsp + 1 cup)

- Oat or soy milk: 1 ½ cups (½ cup + 1 cup)
- Granola: 3 tbsp (2 tbsp + 1 tsp)
- Muesli: ½ cup
- Whole wheat tortilla wraps: 4 (1 + 2 small + 1)
- Whole wheat pasta: 1 cup
- Breadcrumbs: ¼ cup
- Chicken broth: ¾ cup (¼ cup + ½ cup)
- Vegetable broth: 3 cups

Herbs, Spices, Condiments, and Oils
- Olive oil: 3 tbsp (1 tbsp + 1 tbsp + 1 tbsp)
- Unsalted butter: 3 tbsp (2 tbsp + 1 tbsp)
- Light mayonnaise: 4 tbsp (2 tbsp x2)
- Manuka honey: 3 tbsp (1 tbsp + 1 tsp + 1 tsp)
- Acacia honey: 1 tbsp
- Dijon mustard sauce: 1 tbsp
- Hot sauce: 1 tsp
- Balsamic vinegar: 2 tsp (1 tsp x2)
- Lime juice: 6 tsp (1 tbsp + 1 tsp x5)
- Lemon juice: 1 tbsp
- Cumin powder: 1 ½ tsp (½ tsp + 1 tsp)
- Coriander powder: ½ tsp
- Cinnamon powder: 1 tsp (½ tsp x2)
- Cayenne pepper: ¼ tsp
- Paprika powder: 1 ½ tsp (¼ tsp + 1 tsp + ¼ tsp)
- Red chili powder: 1 tsp
- Salt: to taste
- Black pepper: 1 ½ tsp (1/8 tsp x4)
- Garlic powder: pinch
- Dill: ¼ tsp
- Thyme: 1 tsp
- Parsley: 3 tbsp (2 tbsp + 1 tsp)

WEEK 5

Fruits and Vegetables
- Fresh baby spinach leaves: 1 ¼ cups (½ cup + ½ cup + ¼ cup)

- Cherry tomatoes: 2 ¾ cups (½ cup + 1 ¼ cups + 1 cup)
- Red bell pepper: ½ cup (¼ cup + ¼ cup)
- Broccoli florets: ¾ cup (¼ cup + ½ cup)
- Feta cheese: ¼ cup
- Black olives: 1 tbsp
- Zucchini: 2 ½ cups (1 chopped + ½ chopped + 1 sliced)
- Cucumber: 2 cups (1 medium + ¼ cup)
- Mixed veggies: ½ cup (broccoli, carrot, bell peppers)
- Purple cabbage: ½ cup
- Green cabbage: ½ cup
- Green onion: 1, chopped
- Fresh cilantro leaves: 3 tbsp (few leaves + 2 tbsp)
- Fresh raspberries: ¾ cup (¼ cup x3)
- Fresh blueberries: 1 ¼ cups (½ cup + ¼ cup + ½ cup)
- Fresh mango chunks: ½ cup
- Avocado: ½, chopped
- Diced tomato: 1
- Fresh lettuce leaves: to taste
- Eggplant: ½, diced
- Sweet potato puree: 1 cup
- Strawberries: 1 cup (¼ cup + ½ cup)
- Kiwis: 2, peeled and cubed
- Peaches: 2 large, sliced or chopped
- Fuji apple: 1 ½ (1 chopped + ½ diced)
- Medjool dates: 7-8
- Garlic: 3 cloves (1 minced + 1 clove + 1 clove)
- Onions: 2 (1 sliced + 1 chopped + 1 minced)
- Fresh chives: ½ tbsp, chopped

Proteins
- Grilled turkey breast: 9 slices (3 slices x3)
- Chicken breasts: 2
- Tofu: ½
- Canned salmon: 1 can
- Canned tuna: 1 can
- Chickpeas: 2 ¾ cups (¼ cup boiled + ½ cup cooked + 1 cup canned)

- Black beans: ½ cup, rinsed
- Scallops: 6
- Eggs: 4 medium (2 + 2)

Seeds and Nuts

- Chia seeds: 3 ½ tbsp (1 tbsp + 2.5 tbsp)
- Walnuts: 30 g (5 g x6)
- Pecans: 15 g (5 g x3)
- Almonds: 20 g (5 g x4)
- Sunflower seeds: 1 tsp
- Cashews: 5 g
- Brazil nuts: 10 g (5 g x2)
- Flaxseeds: 2 tsp (1 tsp + 1 tsp)
- Pumpkin seeds: 2 tbsp
- Sesame seeds: 2 tbsp

Cereals and Starches

- Rolled oats: 3 ¼ cups (½ cup + 1 cup + 1 ½ cups)
- Whole wheat tortilla wraps: 3 (1 + 2 small)
- Almond flour: ¼ cup
- Granola: ¼ cup
- Oats: ¼ cup
- Almond or soy milk: 2 cups (1 cup + 1 cup)
- Spring water: ¾ cup (¼ cup + ¼ cup + ¼ cup)
- Chocolate-flavored protein powder: 2 tbsp
- Sweet potato puree: 1 cup

Herbs, Spices, Condiments, and Oils

- Extra virgin olive oil: 5 tbsp (1 tbsp + 2 tbsp + 1 tbsp + 1 tbsp)
- Light mayonnaise: 4 tbsp (2 tbsp x2)
- Dijon mustard sauce: 1 tbsp
- Hot sauce: 1 tsp
- Balsamic vinegar: 2 tsp (1 tsp x2)
- Lime juice: 6 tbsp (1 tbsp + 2 tbsp + 1 tbsp + 1 tbsp + 1 tbsp)
- Paprika: 1 ½ tsp (1 tsp + ½ tsp)
- Cumin powder: 1 tsp
- Red chili powder: 1 tsp
- Garlic powder: 1 ¼ tsp (½ tsp + ¼ tsp + ½ tsp)

- Sea salt: to taste
- Black pepper: 1 ¾ tsp (¼ tsp + ½ tsp + 1 tsp)
- Dill: ¼ tsp
- Cardamom powder: pinch
- Cinnamon powder: ½ tsp
- Raw honey: 3 tbsp (2 tbsp + 1 tbsp)

WEEK 6

Fruits and Vegetables

- Mango chunks: ½ cup
- Avocados: 2 (½ cup chopped + ½ ripe sliced)
- Strawberries: 1 ½ cups (½ cup halved + ¼ cup + ¼ cup sliced)
- Blueberries: 1 1/2 cups (¼ cup + 1 cup + ¼ cup)
- Raspberries: 1 cup (½ cup + ½ cup)
- Blackberries: 1 cup
- Pomegranate seeds: 1 cup (½ cup + ½ cup)
- Banana: 1 (½ small sliced + ½ small diced)
- Kiwi: 1 medium
- Pear: 1 medium
- Grapes: ¼ cup red grapes
- Plum tomato: 1
- Fuji apples: 2 medium (1 sliced + 1 chopped)
- Oranges: 2 large, segmented
- Zucchinis: 3 medium
- Cucumbers: 1 chopped
- Cauliflower: 1 head (½ cup cooked + ½ head)
- Beets: 2 medium (1 chopped + 1 chopped)
- Red bell pepper: ¼ cup
- Broccoli florets: ¼ cup
- Baby spinach leaves: 2 ½ cups (½ cup + ½ cup + ½ cup + ½ cup + ½ cup)
- Arugula: 1 ½ cups (½ cup + ½ cup + ½ cup)
- Onions: 4 medium (1 small chopped + ½ sliced + 1 medium chopped + ½ chopped)
- Green onion: 1 chopped
- Garlic: 6-7 cloves (1 whole + 1 minced + 1 minced + 1 clove + 2-3 cloves)
- Fresh basil: to taste

- Fresh parsley: 1 ½ tbsp
- Fresh thyme: 1 tbsp
- Cilantro leaves: a few

Proteins
- Eggs: 2 medium
- Lamb chop: 1
- Chicken breasts: 4 (2 chicken breasts + 1 chicken breast + 1 chicken breast)
- Skinless chicken thighs: 2
- Canned salmon: 1 can
- Chickpeas: 1 cup (½ cup cooked + ½ cup canned)
- Black beans: 1 cup (½ cup rinsed + ¼ cup canned)

Seeds and Nuts
- Almonds: ½ cup + 5 g crushed
- Pecans: 5 g
- Walnuts: 5 g
- Brazil nuts: 5 g
- Pumpkin seeds: ¼ cup
- Sunflower seeds: ¼ cup
- Flaxseeds: 2 tbsp + 1 tsp
- Chia seeds: 3 ½ tbsp
- Sesame seeds: 1 tbsp
- Nut butter: 1 tbsp of your choice

Cereals and Starches
- Quinoa: 2 cups (½ cup cooked + ½ cup + ¼ cup cooked + ½ cup cooked)
- Rolled oats: 1 cup + 2 tbsp
- Whole wheat tortillas: 2
- Muesli: ¼ cup + 1 tbsp
- Granola: 1 tsp
- Graham crackers: ¼ cup
- Almond milk: 200 ml
- Soy milk: 1 ½ cups (1 cup unsweetened + ½ cup)

Herbs, Spices, Condiments, and Oils
- Sea salt: to taste
- Black pepper: to taste
- Cumin powder: 2 tsp (½ tsp + 1 tsp)

- Coriander powder: ½ tsp
- Cinnamon powder: 1 ½ tsp (½ tsp + pinch)
- Cayenne pepper: ¼ tsp
- Red chili flakes: ¼ tsp
- Garlic powder: ¼ tsp (⅛ tsp + 1/8 tsp)
- Paprika: 1 ½ tsp (½ tsp + 1 tsp)
- Dried thyme: 1 tsp
- Lime juice: 7 tbsp (1 tbsp + 2 tbsp + 1 tbsp + 1 tbsp + 1 tbsp + juice of 1 lime)
- Lemon juice: 1 tbsp
- Raw honey: 4 tbsp (1 tbsp + 1 tsp + 1 tbsp + 1 tbsp)
- Acacia honey: 1 tbsp
- Balsamic vinegar: 3 tbsp (2 tbsp + 1 tsp)
- Tahini: 2 tbsp
- Tomato sauce: ¼ cup
- Marinara sauce: ¼ cup
- Low-fat mayonnaise: 2 tbsp
- Extra virgin olive oil: 6 tbsp (1 tsp + 1 tbsp + 1 tbsp + 1 tbsp + 1 tbsp + 1 tbsp)

WEEK 7

Fruits and Vegetables
- Blueberries: 1 cup (fresh or frozen)
- Banana: ½ small (2 in total)
- Apricots (dried): ½ cup
- Granny Smith apple: 1 medium
- Fuji apple: 1 medium
- Peaches: 2 medium
- Plum tomato: 1
- Pomegranate seeds: ½ cup
- Mango chunks: 1 cup (fresh or canned)
- Mango: ½ (diced)
- Kiwis: 2 (peeled and cubed)
- Valencia oranges: 2 large (peeled and segmented)
- Raspberries: ½ cup
- Cherry tomatoes: 1 cup (chopped)
- Pear: 1 medium

- Cauliflower florets: 1 cup
- Baby spinach leaves: ¼ cup (multiple uses, total 2 cups)
- Zucchini: ½ medium (2 in total)
- Red or yellow bell pepper: ¼ cup
- Onion: ½ cup (chopped)
- Tomatoes: ½ cup (chopped)
- Lettuce leaves: ½ cup (chopped)
- Cucumber: ¼ cup (chopped)
- Beet: 1 medium (chopped)
- Broccoli florets: 1 cup
- Brussels sprouts: ½ cup (chopped)
- Baby kale leaves: ¼ cup (chopped)
- Arugula: ¼ cup
- Asparagus spears: 2 (trimmed and chopped)
- Eggplant: ½ (diced)
- Garlic: 3 cloves (minced)
- Fresh basil: ¼ cup
- Cilantro leaves: ¼ cup (fresh)

Proteins

- Chicken breasts: 2 (1 large + 1 small)
- Ground turkey: 100 g
- Scallops: 6
- Chickpeas (canned, rinsed): ½ cup
- Red kidney beans (canned): ½ cup
- White kidney beans (canned): ½ cup
- Black beans (canned): ½ cup
- Boiled chickpeas (canned): ½ cup
- Eggs: 2 medium

Seeds and Nuts

- Flaxseeds: 1 tsp
- Hazelnuts: 5 g
- Walnuts: 5 g (multiple uses)
- Pecans: 5 g (multiple uses)
- Cashews: 5 g
- Shredded coconut: 2 tbsp

- Sesame seeds: 1 tbsp
- Chia seeds: 2 tsp (soaked)
- Tahini: 2 tbsp
- Acacia honey: 1 tbsp
- Raw honey: 1 tbsp

Cereals and Starches

- Whole wheat pasta: 1 cup (any shape)
- Oat flour: 1 cup
- Muesli: ½ cup (no added sugar)
- Whole wheat tortilla wrap: 1 (multiple uses)
- Rice (brown or white): 1 cup
- Cooked quinoa: ½ cup (multiple uses)

Herbs, Condiments, Spices, and Oils

- Unsalted butter: 2 tbsp
- All-purpose flour: 2 tbsp
- Chicken broth: ½ cup (multiple uses)
- Almond milk: ½ cup (multiple uses)
- Almond yogurt: ¼ cup (multiple uses)
- Feta cheese: ¼ cup
- Greek yogurt: ¼ cup
- Light mayonnaise: 1 tbsp
- Dijon mustard: 1 tbsp
- Hot sauce: 1 tsp
- Balsamic vinegar: 1 tsp
- Olive oil: 1 tbsp (multiple uses)
- Extra virgin olive oil: 1 tsp (multiple uses)
- Lemon juice: 1 tbsp
- Lime juice: 2 tbsp (multiple uses)
- Paprika powder: ¼ tsp
- Black pepper: ¼ tsp (multiple uses)
- Salt: to taste (multiple uses)
- Sea salt: ¼ tsp (multiple uses)
- Dried oregano: ¼ tsp
- Dried thyme: 1 tsp
- Cinnamon powder: ½ tsp (multiple uses)

- Red chili flakes: ½ tsp
- Garlic powder: 1/8 tsp
- Vanilla extract: 2 tsp
- Honey: 2 tbsp
- Worcestershire sauce: 1 tbsp
- Corn flour: 1 tsp
- Nutmeg powder: ¼ tsp
- Poppy seeds: 1 tsp
- Stevia: 1 tsp

WEEK 8

Fruits and Vegetables

- Valencia oranges: 2 large (peeled and segmented)
- Arugula: ½ cup
- Baby spinach leaves: 1 ½ cups (multiple uses)
- Fuji apple: 1 medium (sliced)
- Balsamic vinegar: 3 tbsp (2 tbsp + 1 tsp)
- Raw honey: 2 tbsp (1 tsp + 1 tbsp)
- Cooked quinoa: 1 cup (½ cup + ½ cup cooked)
- Black beans: ½ cup (rinsed)
- Chickpeas: 1 ½ cups (½ cup canned + ½ cup cooked + ½ cup rinsed)
- Fresh mango chunks: ½ cup
- Avocado: 1 ½ cups (½ cup chopped + ½ ripe sliced)
- Lime juice: 4 tbsp (1 tbsp + 2 tbsp + 1 tbsp)
- Sea salt: pinch (multiple uses)
- Black pepper: 1 ½ tsp (¼ tsp + ¼ tsp + 1 tsp)
- Cilantro leaves: a few
- Mahi-mahi fillet: 1
- Olive oil: 3 tsp (1 tsp + 1 tbsp + 1 tsp)
- Minced garlic: 2 cloves (1 clove + 1 clove)
- Oregano: 2 tsp (1 tsp + 1 teaspoon dried)
- Red onions: ¼ cup
- Lemon juice: 2 tbsp (1 tbsp + 1 tbsp)
- Medjool dates: 5-6
- Dried cherries: ¼ cup

- Dried raisins: ¼ cup
- Dried figs: ¼ cup
- Walnuts: ¼ cup (multiple uses)
- Granola: 4 tbsp (2 tbsp + 2 tbsp)
- Almond yogurt: 1 cup
- Raspberries: ½ cup
- Blueberries: 1 ¼ cups (½ cup + ¼ cup + ½ cup)
- Kiwis: 2 (peeled and cubed)
- Chia seeds: 5 tsp (2 tsp soaked + 1 tbsp + 2 tsp)
- Manuka honey: 1 tbsp (for drizzling)
- Chicken breasts: 2 (1 large + 1 small)
- Extra virgin olive oil: 2 tbsp (1 tbsp + 1 tbsp)
- Broccoli florets: 1 ½ cups (1 cup + ½ cup)
- Brussels sprouts: ½ cup (chopped)
- Red chili flakes: ½ tsp
- Sesame seeds: 1 tsp
- Rice (brown or white): 1 cup
- Honey: 2 tbsp
- Chicken broth: ½ cup (¼ cup + ¼ cup)
- Sesame oil: 1 tbsp
- Paprika powder: ½ tsp (¼ tsp + ¼ tsp)
- Worcestershire sauce: 1 tbsp
- Corn flour: 1 tsp
- Ground turkey: 100g
- Egg: 1
- Zucchinis: 3 (1 spiralized + 2 medium + 1 cup chopped)
- Breadcrumbs: ¼ cup
- Low-sugar marinara sauce: ⅓ cup
- Parsley: 2 tbsp (1 tbsp chopped + 1 tbsp)
- Grated parmesan cheese: 3 tbsp
- Rolled oats: ¼ cup
- Soy milk: 1 cup (unsweetened)
- Spring water: ¼ cup
- Vanilla extract: 2 tsp
- Graham crackers: ¼ cup (store-bought)

- Almonds: 10 g (5 g chopped + 5 g whole)
- Flaxseeds: 3 tsp (1 tsp + 1 tsp + 1 tsp)
- Strawberries: 1 cup (fresh or frozen)
- Eggplant: ½ (diced)
- Tomatoes: ½ cup (sliced + 1 diced)
- Cranberries: ½ cup
- Mint leaves: ¼ cup
- Stevia: 1 tsp
- Ice cubes: as needed
- Cucumber: 2 ½ cups (1 medium chopped + 1 cup chopped + ½ cucumber diced)
- Cherry tomatoes: 1 cup (chopped)
- Romaine lettuce leaves: ½ cup (chopped)
- Tofu: ½
- Mixed veggies: ½ cup (broccoli, carrot, bell peppers)
- Dark chocolate chips: ⅛ cup
- Peanut butter: ¼ cup
- Raw honey: ⅛ cup
- Ground flaxseeds: ⅛ cup
- Cardamom powder: pinch (multiple uses)
- Nutmeg powder: pinch
- Hemp seeds: 2 tbsp

Proteins

- Chicken breasts: 2 (1 large + 1 small)
- Ground turkey: 100 g
- Egg: 1
- Mahi-mahi fillet: 1
- Tofu: ½

Cereals and Starches

- Whole wheat pasta: 1 cup (any shape)
- Cooked quinoa: 1 cup (½ cup + ½ cup cooked)
- Rolled oats: ¼ cup
- Rice (brown or white): 1 cup
- Granola: 4 tbsp (2 tbsp + 2 tbsp)

Seeds and Nuts

- Pecans: 10 g (5 g crushed + 5 g whole)

- Poppy seeds: 1 tsp
- Walnuts: ¼ cup (multiple uses)
- Almonds: 10 g (5 g chopped + 5 g whole)
- Chia seeds: 5 tsp (2 tsp soaked + 1 tbsp + 2 tsp)
- Flaxseeds: 3 tsp (1 tsp + 1 tsp + 1 tsp)
- Hemp seeds: 2 tbsp
- Sesame seeds: 1 tsp

Herbs, Condiments, Spices, and Oils

- Olive oil: 3 tsp (1 tsp + 1 tbsp + 1 tsp)
- Extra virgin olive oil: 2 tbsp (1 tbsp + 1 tbsp)
- Balsamic vinegar: 3 tbsp (2 tbsp + 1 tsp)
- Raw honey: 2 tbsp (1 tbsp + 1 tbsp)
- Sesame oil: 1 tbsp
- Worcestershire sauce: 1 tbsp
- Corn flour: 1 tsp
- Sea salt: pinch (multiple uses)
- Black pepper: 1 ½ tsp (¼ tsp + ¼ tsp + 1 tsp)
- Paprika powder: ½ tsp (¼ tsp + ¼ tsp)
- Red chili flakes: ½ tsp
- Dried oregano: 1 tsp
- Fresh basil: ¼ cup (multiple uses)

REFERENCES

- Bender, D. A., & Cunningham, S. M. (2021). *Introduction to nutrition and metabolism.* CRC Press.

- Gropper, S. S., & Smith, J. L. (2013). *Advanced nutrition and human metabolism.* Cengage Learning.

- Lanham-New, S. A., Macdonald, I. A., & Roche, H. M. (Eds.). (2011). *Nutrition and metabolism.* John Wiley & Sons.

- Proestos, C. (2018). Superfoods: Recent data on their role in the prevention of diseases. *Current Research in Nutrition and Food Science Journal, 6*(3), 576-593.

- Arumugam, T., Sona, C. L., & Maheswari, M. U. (2021). Fruits and vegetables as Superfoods: Scope and demand. *J. Pharm. Innov, 10,* 119-129.

- Fernández-Ríos, A., Laso, J., Hoehn, D., Amo-Setién, F. J., Abajas-Bustillo, R., Ortego, C., ... & Margallo, M. (2022). A critical review of superfoods from a holistic nutritional and environmental approach. *Journal of Cleaner Production, 379,* 134491.

- Gencer, B., Marston, N. A., Im, K., Cannon, C. P., Sever, P., Keech, A., ... & Sabatine, M. S. (2020). Efficacy and safety of lowering LDL cholesterol in older patients: a systematic review and meta-analysis of randomized controlled trials. *The Lancet, 396*(10263), 1637-1643.

- Brautbar, A., & Ballantyne, C. M. (2011). Pharmacological strategies for lowering LDL cholesterol: statins and beyond. *Nature Reviews Cardiology, 8*(5), 253-265.

- Bruckert, E., & Rosenbaum, D. (2011). Lowering LDL cholesterol through diet: potential role in the statin era. *Current opinion in lipidology, 22*(1), 43-48.

- Qaid, M. M., & Abdelrahman, M. M. (2016). Role of insulin and other related hormones in energy metabolism—A review. *Cogent Food & Agriculture, 2*(1), 1267691.

- Miers, W. R., & Barrett, E. J. (1998). The role of insulin and other hormones in the regulation of amino acid and protein metabolism in humans. *Journal of Basic and Clinical Physiology and Pharmacology, 9*(2-4), 235-254.

RECIPE INDEX

Blueberry Banana Smoothie   37
Strawberry Almond Oats Smoothie   37
Mixed Berries Smoothie Fusion   38
Green Avocado Smoothie   38
Creamy Spinach and Pear Smoothie   39
Strawberry Smoothie Bowl with nuts and granola   39
Quinoa High-Protein Breakfast Bowl 40
Overnight Chia seeds Breakfast Bowl 40
Oatmeal Breakfast Bowl   41
Scrambled Eggs and Veggie Breakfast Bowl   41
Hard Boiled Eggs Veggie Salad   42
Almond Yogurt Parfait With Assorted Fruits 42
Overnight Oatmeal High-Fiber Breakfast   43
Cinnamon Sweet Potato Oatmeal Pancakes   43
Muesli and Oatmeal Waffle With Apricots   44
Sesame Chicken with Sauteed Veggies   46
Garlic Salmon Patties With Coleslaw Salad   46
Whole Wheat Tuna Wrap   47
Grilled Turkey And Veggie Wrap   47
Quinoa Black Bean Salad With Lime Dressing   48
Green Spinach Pasta With Creamy Parmesan Sauce 48
Peach And Avocado Salad With Feta Cheese Topping   49
Blueberry And Arugula Salad With Cheese   49
Crunchy Strawberry Spinach Salad   50
Mixed Beans And Veggie Salad   50
Edamame Beans Cucumber Kale Salad   51
Grilled Chicken Breast With Avocado And Pomegranate Seeds   51
Broccoli Veggie Pasta Salad With Pine Nuts   52
Greek Turkey Lettuce Rolls   54
Seared Scallops With Spinach   54
Chicken Zucchini Frittata Casserole   55
Grilled Mahi-Mahi With Mango Salsa   55
Slow-Cooked Lemon Basil Chicken   56
Slow-Cooked Chicken Fajitas 56
Eggplant And Chickpea Stew 57
Grilled Tofu And Quinoa Bowl   57

Moroccan Lamb With Cauliflower Rice 58
Slow-cooked barbecue Chicken 58
Avocado Tuna Salad 59
Turkey Meatballs With Zucchini Noodles 59
Herbed Chicken Thighs With Cauliflower Mash 60
Homemade Flaxseed And Oats Energy-Rich Bars 62
Homemade Mixed Nuts And Muesli Energy Bites 62
Homemade Dates And Dried Cherries Energy Bars 63
Homemade Dates And Dried Fruits Energy Bars 63
Homemade Almond And Oats Energy Bars 64
Oats And Hemp Seeds Energy Bites 64
Oats And Peach Fusion Smoothie 65
Fiber-Rich Almond Chocolate Smoothie Bowl 65
Lime And Paprika-Seasoned Chickpeas 66
Almond Raspberry Smoothie 66
Banana Oatmeal Cookies 67
Quinoa And Chia Seeds Energy Bites With Berries 67
Healthy Fiber-Rich Fruits Salad Bowl 68
Golden Turmeric Cinnamon-Infused Milk 70
Lemon and Ginger-infused Tea 70
Lemon-infused Rosemary Tea 71
Mint-infused Fenugreek Seeds Tea 71
Orange-Infused Oolong Iced Tea 72
Lemon-infused Ginkgo Biloba Tea 72
Energy Blast Strawberry Drink 73
Mango Oats Smoothie 73
Pomegranate and Beet Drink 74
Refreshing Lime and Cherry Drink 74
Green Booster Energy Drink 75
Tropical Pineapple Energy Drink 75
Citrusy Peach Smoothie 76
Green Broccoli Salad With Olives And Lime Dressing 78
Spinach Arugula Pear Salad With Walnuts 78
Citrusy Detox Green Smoothie 79
Lime-Infused Chickpea Mint Avocado Bowl 79
Whole Wheat Quinoa Wrap With Asparagus And Beans 80
Green Detox Smoothie 80
Orange Arugula Pecan Salad With Balsamic Vinegar Dressing 81
Cauliflower Kale Chickpea Bowl With Parsley 81

Spinach Beet Quinoa Detox Salad   82
Zucchini Basil-Infused Soup 82
Cranberry Detox Mint Juice 83
Broccoli And Zucchini Salad with Olive Oil Dill Dressing   83
Blackberry Arugula Salad with Cashews   83

Printed in Great Britain
by Amazon